Achieving Classroom Confidence

What You Need to Know to Survive and Thrive as a New Elementary School Teacher

By

Betsy Weigle, M.Ed.

ClassroomCaboodleBooks.com

Dedicated to classroom teachers everywhere.
You put your hearts on the line every day in the
service of children.

~

Thanks to my husband Scott... tireless editor,
layout expert, and brainstormer

Contents

Achieving Classroom Confidence

What You Need to Know to Survive and Thrive as a New Elementary School Teacher

About Betsy

Betsy Weigle has worked in a wide range of education roles: assistant secretary, K-6 substitute teacher, teacher of third, fourth, and fifth grades, and educational technology facilitator. In the process, she has earned a Master's in Education and National Board Certification.

What drives Betsy? Kids. Especially kids with needs: homeless students, students with special needs, and students who face challenges in their personal and family lives.

She created ClassroomCaboodle.com to help new *and* experienced teachers who are on the front lines in elementary education.

Welcome to the World of Teaching

This is the book that I wish had existed when I was training to become a new teacher and taking over my first classroom. There was SO much to learn and so much conflicting advice... it drove me crazy to think that I couldn't find the most critical information in one place. Well, I've taken care of that for you! This is the book that explains:

- Things they will never tell you in college about the way the education system really works.

- How to act as a new teacher so children will *want* to learn from you.

- The fundamentals of getting children to behave.

- The basics of setting up your room effectively without spending too much time *or* money.

- How to schedule, plan, and deliver your lessons.

I've also included a thousand other details I wish someone had told me so I didn't have to learn them all the hard way!

This is the book for first-time teachers starting new jobs *and* pre-service teachers who are just beginning their education journeys.

The "new teacher" phase extends from the junior year of college (when pre-service teachers begin their practicums) clear through the first year or two of taking over one's own classroom. It's a time of intense learning - a critical time for laying a foundation that will ensure that you thrive in this profession rather than burning out and leaving. I want you to stay, because you are desperately needed by children, but you have to know what you are getting yourself into.

College students: My primary focus is on first-year teachers (which you will soon be), but I've included tons of specific advice that will help you through your student-teaching, as well.

In short, if you have made a commitment to becoming not just a teacher, but an amazing, life-changing teacher…

This the book for you.

What This Book Is Not

What to leave in and what to leave out? This is a perennially difficult question for an author, especially a teacher-author who knows (as I do) that *everything* you do in elementary school is connected to *everything else*; you can't teach math if you can't hold children's attention; you can't hold children's attention if you can't plan engaging math lessons. And so on and so on.

I once thought about writing a book with absolutely everything you need to know to be one of the truly great teachers. Then I realized that no one would read a thousand-page book! *I* wouldn't even read it, to tell the truth. Instead, I started my website, ClassroomCaboodle.com, where I have published hundreds of articles and videos... and barely scratched the surface of everything that goes on in an elementary school classroom.

So this book is not "all you need to know." It's a starting point. It will help you avoid some outright surprises and will provide techniques to get you started while you are finding your own way and developing your own teaching style. My fondest hope is that it will guide you toward asking your own questions and seeking your own answers... the same outcome we strive to achieve with our students.

Besides the information on my website, I do have other books, some in progress as of this writing and others already complete. You can find my books on Amazon or at this link: www.ClassroomCaboodleBooks.com

Your FREE Resources

Speaking of my website, I have set up a page there that is just for the readers of this book. You can access it at this link:

www.ClassroomCaboodle.com/NewTeacher

Here is what you'll find there:

- Helpful videos

- Free downloads
- Recommended resources for new teachers
- Discount coupon for my store

I love my teacher readers, and I'm happy to provide these extra items especially for you!

Who Chooses Teaching?

Is elementary school teaching your ideal career? How do you *know?*

Well... you bought this book, didn't you? Anyone who buys a book with this title has already revealed themselves as being drawn to the education of children. You see, becoming a teacher is a calling first, and a process second. Just consider the job description:

The ideal candidate will enjoy managing the behavior of 20 to 30 young children from a wide variety of social and economic backgrounds for six hours a day while being responsible for teaching the following subjects to mastery:

- Reading
- Writing
- Spelling
- Math

- Social Studies
- Science
- Technology

That will eliminate a very large percentage of adults - and most of the rest will run for the hills after reading the next part:

In addition to academic instruction and behavior management, this position requires the ability to help children daily with:

- Learning disabilities
- Hygiene
- Social skills
- Making friends
- Boy/girl relationships
- Any issues they bring from home

Hello? Anyone left in the line to sign up? Oh, good - you're still here! And that's how you *know* that you want to be a teacher: this list doesn't scare you, it makes you want to get started.

People are *called* to teaching because it has a job description unlike any other career. I can tell already that you've been "called." And what's more, you want to be the teacher whose name kids remember for the rest of their lives - the kind of classroom teacher that our children deserve.

Changing the World One Child at a Time

I truly believe that the world is changed one child at a time. Not only are kids' individual lives affected by what we do every day, but additionally, these kids then go out and make their mark on the world based on what they learn in school. Is there any other profession that has that kind of impact?

I don't think so!
However, this realization that our students' futures depend on what we teach them in school comes with a very profound responsibility: children cannot lose a single year of learning, or they may be set back for their entire lives.

This means that even brand-new teachers have to hit the ground running; taking a year or two to figure out how to effectively teach math, reading, and writing may mean that several dozen children don't make adequate yearly progress and therefore struggle in future grades.

Of course, some kids can bounce back from a year of poor instruction - after all, many of us can recall a few inefficient teachers in our pasts, and we turned out okay. But there are plenty of kids who are not intellectually or socioeconomically well-prepared to endure even a single year of inadequate instruction, and these are the kids who need the full benefits of education the most.

Which is why…

We Need You!

There is a critical need for teachers who truly love their work and want to teach children, build them up, and set them on a path to success. As far as I'm concerned, the future is lost without people like you. That's not to say that everyone feels that way!

Teachers often get criticized in our society. But that proves my point, I think: the public is not getting overly excited about hairstylists or plumbers. But when peoples' kids are involved, they care deeply. Beyond what *parents* want for their own children, *society* expects you to educate the next generation for the good of the country... which is why politicians are so deeply involved in education (and often so critical of our profession).

That's all kind of big picture, though, and hard to wrap our minds around. More importantly, you'll find when you enter your classroom that *individual* students need you to teach and nurture them for the good of their personal self-esteem and development. Sometimes all of those voices out there harping on "how to improve our schools" can start to blur together and lose their urgency. I mean, how are we supposed to accomplish a huge task like improving the education system? It's too big to grasp. But when you consider that little girl tugging on your hand and asking again if you can explain counting by threes... now that's a responsibility we can understand.

So when I say that "we" need you, I'm really speaking on behalf of your future students. If you take care of them, all the rest of it falls in line.

The Recipe for Success

Make no mistake: There are awesome teachers, great teachers, good teachers, not-so-good teachers, and awful teachers. You experienced all types during your years in school, didn't you? I know I did! When I decided to get my teaching degree, I determined that I wanted to be one of the great ones. And maybe, if I tried hard enough, I might even be considered "awesome" by at least a few students. I know you have the same goal.

Here's the thing: I learned over the years that being "good" and even "great" often just takes time and dedication. But "awesome"... that takes a little special sauce. This book is about mixing up that sauce right from the beginning, even before you finish college.

Be warned: It's not an easy recipe! There are a lot of ingredients. But the difference between great food and amazing food has always taken inspired cooking. Not everyone is naturally that kind of cook, but when you know the exact ingredients to add and the precise steps to take, suddenly you have a huge advantage and a shot at serving something amazing - or nearly amazing, at least - on your first try.

I'm going to share one secret with you right now, one ingredient in this recipe that will form the basis for the rest of the book. It's the number-one, critical thing you need to know because it will give you confidence for all that follows. Here it is:

Every one of your elementary students WANTS you to be super-successful. From the first moment they look at you, they desperately want you to be the kind of teacher they can love with all their hearts and respect with all their minds.

It's true. And it makes everything you are about to learn a lot easier to implement than you may think. Here's what we are going to cover...

Step-by-Step In Your Classroom

We are going to cover your road map for teaching in five parts. Here they are:

Part 1. Teaching: Reality vs. Romance

- What makes a good teacher? Are good teachers born or made?

- What you need to know about the education "system"

- Your first classroom experiences - pitfalls and opportunities

Part 2. Building a Community of Learners

- Taking center stage in your classroom - capturing attention and building your fan club

- Creating and nurturing teacher/student relationships

- Basic strategies for managing behavior

- Caring for the personal needs of your children

Part 3. Classroom Set-up and Organization

- Effectively organizing your classroom

- Important considerations about student desk management

- The basics of student and teacher supplies

- Finding books and managing your classroom library

- How to decorate your room without under- or overdoing it

Part 4. High-Impact Teaching

- Effective lesson planning: Covering it all with rigor and attention to detail

- High-engagement lesson delivery with individualizing built in

- Maximizing success on unit assessments and year-end tests

- Ensuring substitutes are well-prepared to teach in your absence

Part 5. From Zero to Awesome in Record Time

- Super-charging your classroom learning experiences

- How to make connections at school, whom to connect with, and why

- How to interact with parents as partners in learning

- Surviving teacher observations and evaluations without (too much) stress

- Recovering from mistakes with grace and making continual improvement

We've got a lot of ground to cover, but I promise you'll be taking your first steps toward super-teacher status in short order. But first, let me tell you a little story...

My Path to the Classroom

I really wanted the job.

It was a low-income school in one of the poorest neighborhoods in my state. During the interview, the principal asked me this question:

> "What do you want your students to say about you at the end of the school year?"

How would you answer that question? I didn't have to think very long before saying:

> "I would like my kids to say on the last day of school that we worked really, really hard, but they loved every minute of it."

To me, that is the essence of being not just a great teacher, but an amazing teacher: getting kids to work hard at learning and making them love it. You don't change the world by getting kids to like you or even by having a great learning community. Don't get me wrong - those things are critical when it comes to being a super-teacher, and without them, you can't make any real progress in learning.

But to actually change the world through your actions, your students have to learn *a lot* during their time with you.

I got that job, and boy, did I put those kids through their paces! They came from such rough backgrounds, with broken homes and drug use. There were multiple kids with IEP's and learning disabilities. But, together, we dug into every single subject and pushed ourselves beyond anything they thought possible. They got to the point where hard work felt good to them because, at the end of every day, they felt like they had really accomplished something.

At the end of the year, they did great on the state assessments, and I had gotten a lesson in one of the fundamental truths about children: they *want* to learn, and they want their teacher to push them hard to do it.

I'm Here to Help You!

I want you to have a roomful of kids who work their little brains to a frazzle every day and love doing it because they love learning from you. That's the whole reason I started my Classroom Caboodle website; sharing the successful strategies that I have learned in my own classroom is what motivates me. We have a lot of work to do and a lot of children to teach every year. If I can help you reach a few more students, help you push kids to their full potential, then I'll feel that I have been able to give back in a meaningful way to the teaching profession.

Are you ready?

Let's get started by talking about the reality of teaching in today's education world. There can be a lot of hurdles between you and your goal of teaching children, even when you work in a system that is supposed to enable teaching and learning. That's ironic, but true. The good news is that a well-prepared teacher can make any system function to the advantage of students, but you need to be fully aware of how things actually work.

Let's move on to Part 1!

PART 1

Teaching Reality vs. Teaching Romance

The difference between the great and the not-so-great in teaching is rooted in one thing: attitude.

~ Betsy Weigle

Betsy Weigle

Teaching in the Education "System"

Whenever you see a painting of the ancient Greek philosopher Socrates teaching, he's always perched on a rock in the countryside with his students gathered about him like they just finished a picnic. Doesn't that sound idyllic? No rules or restrictions, just a free exchange of ideas and information - the teacher imparting knowledge and young minds soaking it up. Well, Socrates never had to answer to a principal or a school board, but every teacher since him has!

To be honest, I have some hesitation when it comes to writing this section because I'm afraid that it will be a little bit of a downer to idealistic new teachers. But I've been answering questions from new teachers on social media for a long time, and I know that every one of them would really have appreciated a little more background knowledge before being caught up in school politics and bureaucracy. If I don't tell you now, you'll find out on the very first day you show up to school. So let's move forward with the understanding that I'm not trying to discourage you; I'm simply making sure that your eyes are wide open.

Unless you are homeschooling your children, your teaching career will be spent inside of the education System. And yes, that's "System" with a capital "S" because it is a big, complicated machine that will work its way into every detail of your classroom experience and even into many parts of your personal life. Bear in mind that when I'm discussing this system, I am primarily talking about the United States, although I would be very surprised if it doesn't exist in nearly the same form in other countries. I'm also talking about an average of the entire country; you may find that your local district varies in both positive and negative aspects.

My comments in this chapter will be focused mainly upon the public school system since I'm most familiar with it. However, don't fool yourself that a private school system will be much different in the practical impact it has on you and your classroom; I hear from plenty of teachers who work in private schools, and their concerns almost perfectly mirror those who work in public schools.

Let's start by hearing from a brand-new teacher who has suddenly found herself inside a teaching environment that she didn't even know existed when she was job-hunting.

Debra's Story

Recently, I heard from one of my followers who was super-excited about getting job interviews and starting her first position. I gave her advice through that entire process and celebrated with her when she landed her first job as a Special Education teacher.

A few short weeks later, I heard from her again. Her message was filled with a dismaying list of the challenges she had faced. She ended with this question:

"It's only been four weeks, and I can't believe the conditions that they are expecting me to work under. I have all of these kids with IEP's whom I quite literally cannot service because of a lack of Special Education curriculum and the fact that my principal keeps using me as an in-building substitute teacher!

"I hate to say it, but I'm already looking at job openings in different districts. I don't see how it could be much worse, and I don't know if I can spend the whole year working under these conditions.

"What do you think?"

Here's part of my response:

"Debra:

"I'm so sorry that you have had to experience such highs and lows in such a short period of time. Now that you are part of the system, I need to share some thoughts with you.

"Here's the difficult part of teaching: No matter where you go, there will be an administration. And sometimes you'll find admin that is excellent and has the best interests of the kids at heart. And sometimes you'll find admin that considers the kids an unfortunate aspect of running a school. Most often, they'll be somewhere in between: their hearts sort of in the right place but their brains more concerned with politics, appearances, test scores, and budgets than individual student success.

"So, ultimately, you have to do what you think is best. Just be aware that sometimes the fire you are jumping into is as hot as the frying pan you are jumping from!

"I'm sorry that this wonderful opportunity is turning out to be not quite so wonderful. No matter where you teach, all you can do is your best for the individual kids under your care. It will be frustrating because you cannot give them the best services for their needs, but I guarantee that you will make a difference in the lives of several children every single year."

It's because of Debra and all of the hundreds of other teachers whom I have heard from over the years that I'm writing this book. The education system is the result of very complex interactions among a wide variety of factors, many of which are not readily apparent at first glance. So, let's dive deeper into this system and shine some light on how it works.

Why Do So Many People Care?

Teachers will often complain that all they want to do is to be left alone to teach. "Is that so much to ask?" they wonder. Well, frankly, yes, it is.

You see, whether you are working in a public or private school system, you are teaching other people's children. That alone is going to ensure that a whole bunch of adults are going to be in your business, so to speak. When you add in the fact that these adults are paying for the system (including your salary) through taxes or through private tuition payments, then you can be certain that you will never simply be "left alone."

People take the education of children very seriously, and they all – from parents to politicians – have very strong opinions about how it should be accomplished. On one hand, this is great because it means that the public is constantly engaged in the quality of our education system. On the other hand, you will find that there are a lot of people with no classroom experience at all who are firmly convinced that they are better at your job than you are.

How Did We Get Here?

The unfortunate truth is that, in spite of the efforts of the education system for many decades, there has been a lack of results (such as low graduation rates and decreasing math ability) in many portions of the country. This is what is driving the intense pressure that school systems and teachers now feel.

"But wait," you say, "have poor results really been the fault of teachers? Teachers just kept doing what they've always done while society changed around them! You know... single-parent homes, poverty, and everything else that occurs in the great 'melting pot' of the United States."

A very good question. You won't find me saying that teachers had no role to play in the results coming out of their own classrooms, but I will heartily agree that the teaching landscape is infinitely more difficult to navigate than it was a few decades ago. I can't imagine what some of my elementary school teachers would have done if faced with the challenges of a modern classroom! There is lots of blame to go around for the difficulties that our education system has experienced, from changing social values to different concepts about childhood discipline to extensive lack of funding.

Regardless of the causes, the public has demanded huge changes from politicians. Without being certain as to exactly what they want, parents everywhere desire for schools to "work better," and that is precisely what politicians nationwide are setting out to do. In a few states - very few - they are addressing the lack of funding (albeit, not with very much enthusiasm). So, what else can they do to make schools work better? Well, it's pretty obvious that politicians have no control whatsoever over how children are raised at home. In fact, we really don't want them to have any control over that, do we?

So guess who's left directly in the cross-hairs of every policymaker from your local principal up to the President of the United States? You. You are the only thing besides funding that politicians can control. That's why 99% of the stress of improving education outcomes falls upon the classroom teacher. This is not fair, by any stretch of the imagination, but I have thought long and hard about it, and there's really no other approach that "society" can take. There are only a few levers that can be pulled, and the biggest lever in the education machine is labeled "classroom teacher." And, boy, are people lining up to pull it!

The impact on you is that, from the moment you step foot into your first school – even before you get your classroom full of kids – there are going to be a multitude of people who are thoroughly interested in every little thing you do. You will find sky-high expectations and a frustrating lack of time, resources, and support with which to achieve those expectations.

I truly hope that you find a little piece of the system that does not follow this pattern. However, in a long education career, I would bet any amount of money that you will experience your share of system-induced stress.

So much for the background. But it's not enough to know *generalities*. I'm going to take you step-by-step through the *realities* of the education system.

It's Not Always about the Students

The first reality comes from the fact that there is a system in the first place. We have to have systems - they make for efficient delivery of a product, even if that product is the education of children. There have to be people whose job it is to maintain schools, order supplies, and manage payroll, just like in any large corporation. But that means there are a whole bunch of people in the system who are really there just to have a job. It will never be the case that every single person involved in education is passionate about children. It is not human nature for most people to be really passionate about their jobs, even if their jobs are very important to society.

So, what you'll often see is that the system becomes an end in itself - meaning that it exists in order to provide paychecks to the people within it, rather than to fulfill its primary function of educating children.

This is probably the number-one frustration that I hear from teachers: that the system is not about the children, that it's about all that "human" stuff like egos and office politics and appearances. Often, the students are not individuals, but data points. One would hope that the system would be balanced with a large dose of humanity and a sense of purpose, but that is not always the case.

Money Matters

It really, really matters. As in, it matters a whole lot. Can I be any more clear about that?

Budgets control absolutely everything, and there is never enough money in them for the things that you feel really matter. I'll talk more about how this impacts you personally in a moment. Budgets are tricky things because they are always divided up into different buckets of money. One bucket may be completely empty, while another one is still overflowing. That's why you'll never be provided with enough pencils in your classroom, but your school district will spend millions of dollars on brand-new curricula. It seems crazy, but it's the way every business in the world works.

Sometimes districts are restricted on how they can spend certain buckets of money because they've been filled through tax levies or other election-driven processes. Perhaps they've been given grants that come with strings attached. There are all kinds of reasons that money can be spent in large doses in certain places and yet not be available for spending in other places. It's complicated, but you just need to know that, although there's a lot of money sloshing around in the education system, you personally may see evidence of only a few drops in your own classroom.

The mere existence of money in the education system puts extensive pressure on priorities, but that's nothing compared to the pressure that results from a *lack* of money. You see, the general public who care so passionately about education also firmly believe that their taxes should be as low as possible. Yes, this is a contradiction, but there it is. It may not make sense, but it's how things work.

More Money Matters

And now, even more discussion of money... your money!

Think back to your own elementary school classrooms. Remember the cute nametags on the desks, the cheerful themes, the coordinated labels on the book tubs? Do you think your classroom teachers were given a special little pot of money to create those welcoming atmospheres? Yeah... right. Sure, the school probably had some markers lying around or some colored paper, but those decorations you remember were not hacked together with markers and colored paper! They were purchased out-of-pocket by the teacher.

And it's not only decorations. Do you remember those overflowing tubs filled with books to explore? Doesn't that seem like a basic requirement for properly stocking a classroom? Well, of course it does, but I will guarantee that over three-fourths of the general-reading books that you find in any elementary classroom are purchased by the teacher.

The list goes on and on. Teaching is extraordinarily unique in that there is a societal expectation that teachers will spend their own personal money on their professional jobs. More than that, teachers themselves expect to do it, and, although they will complain about it, they will still keep doing it. I have often wondered what would happen if every single teacher in the country refused to spend a dime that was not being reimbursed. Would the plain classrooms and barren bookshelves motivate any political action?

Yes, there is some reimbursement built into the system. It is usually a few hundred dollars available through a Federal tax deduction, and many states and districts do have some stipends that have been negotiated into teacher contracts to help reimburse these out-of-pocket expenditures. But don't kid yourself: these reimbursements will come nowhere close to making up the money that you will spend over the years on creating a safe and effective learning environment for your students.

It's not just on classroom decorations and books that you'll be spending money; you will find that it's difficult to get funding for something as basic as pencils or hand sanitizer. You may be lucky enough to have supportive parents who will gladly provide classroom items, but you may very well find yourself working in schools where parental support is nonexistent, and, if you want these items in your classroom, you will end up paying for them.

You'll do it because you won't be able to bear the thought of children coming to school and spending six hours in non-optimal conditions. A cynic might suggest that your administration is relying on that; they know that you will be driven by your heart to create an ideal classroom environment, even if they don't help you pay for it.

And still the outflow of money won't stop. In addition to decorations, books, and basic supplies, you will find yourself seriously considering paying for curricula. If you have not heard of Teachers Pay Teachers, you soon will. It's an open marketplace for teachers to sell lesson plans, etc., to other teachers. I have almost 250 education items listed there myself, and you'll see when you click through to the free resources page that the same items are for sale in my own online store.

I am very honored that teachers consider my supplies to be helpful in the classroom and that they are willing to pay for them. But I also understand that it seems crazy that the curriculum provided to these teachers is so inadequate that they feel they must supplement by paying out of their own pockets in order to properly teach their children.

But, again, those kids who look at you for six hours every day, expecting you to work miracles, will be all the justification you need to spend your latté money on multiplication worksheets. Well, let's be honest: it's not only the children who will drive you to pay for your own curricula - tests and accountability will provide just as much motivation. More on that in a bit.

Personal Time Investment

On your next available weekend, I invite you to drive by the parking lots of three or four schools in your city. In every one of those parking lots, you will see cars. And that means there are teachers inside the buildings working on the weekend to get ready for the coming week. You can take the same drive in July or August, and you'll see teachers working during summer break in order to prepare for the coming year.

You will find yourself doing exactly the same thing, no matter how much you commit to not doing it. That's because there are way more tasks to accomplish during the school day or school week than can possibly be accomplished given the time available. So, what gets squeezed out of the school day and into your weekend is prep and planning. Oh, and don't forget the stacks of papers to correct nearly every night after dinner!

You see, in our modern system, teachers are expected to teach so many things that there is literally not enough time to teach it all, which is why you will end up donating fairly large portions of your personal time to your career. Don't ever fool yourself – or let your friends tell you – that teachers work part-time jobs and get all kinds of time off. Yes, it is nice to get those long holidays and summer breaks. But you're not getting paid for those breaks, and you are still going to be working during them.

With time and experience - often a few years - this will moderate itself. If your curriculum remains stable, you will become an expert in efficiently preparing to teach it. But all bets are off when new standards or new curricula are rolled out! Inevitably, you will see your time spent on preparation rise.

Nonstop Testing

You will be amazed at how many tests your children are expected to take - it can literally be five tests within the first three days of school. And it never relents after that.

School systems across the country have suddenly discovered *data*. After many decades of essentially ignoring data or failing to collect it in an accurate fashion, they have jumped wholeheartedly on board with the trends you see in every other business in America. Results matter, and, in order to understand whether results are being achieved, you must measure. Thus, testing.

The testing, of course, has two purposes. The first is to make an attempt at ensuring that students are actually making progress. The second – which relates to the discussion above about the focus on teachers – is to hold teachers accountable for this student progress.

It will likely take many years before the education system becomes experienced enough with data collection to do it in a sophisticated manner that is not applied like a hammer to our young students. In the meantime, you will need to brace yourself for the reality of testing and, in spite of any personal feelings you may develop, not take it out on your children. I discuss assessments later in this book.

All of these tests are based on standards...

Standards, Standards, And More Standards

Standards in some form are here to stay. Many people have very strong opinions regarding the Common Core State Standards. I personally am a proponent, and nearly all of my products are closely correlated with them. Common Core has gotten a lot of bad press for the consequences (testing) that it causes and some of the ill-conceived curricula that publishers have produced. But the standards themselves are a pretty comprehensive effort to gather in one spot everything a child should know from kindergarten through twelfth grade in reading, writing, and math.

Still, I'll grant that reasonable minds can disagree. However, disagree or not, you'll find that you have no choice whatsoever in implementing them or other some other set of standards adopted by your state. Standards in some form are here to stay, if for no other reason than the common-sense notion that ten-year-olds across the country should be learning generally the same thing at the same time... and, frankly, should be learning at the same or higher level than ten-year-olds in other countries.

As I outline in one of my other books, *Elementary Einsteins: Four Simple Steps to Challenging Gifted Kids in your Classroom*, Common Core standards do make it much simpler to individualize and challenge your students.

Nonstop Changes

Change will be your constant companion throughout your teaching career. It's been a long time since a teacher could pull out her well-worn lesson plans and repeat the same thing she had done for years. It is highly likely that you will be experiencing a moderate level of change in curriculum, methodology, or priorities every single year and a significant amount of change at least once every three years.

My biggest recommendation is to make the commitment that you won't be dragged kicking and screaming every step of the way! Change is inevitable, and getting on board as quickly as possible will lessen the stress on you.

If it's any consolation, you can discuss the rate of change with your friends who work for profit-making corporations. Be warned, however, that they will not have much sympathy for you!

Technology Integration

You will need to become very comfortable with technology integration. Having worked many years as a technology facilitator, I can tell you that this is probably one of the biggest difficulties teachers have. And this isn't exclusive to teachers who have been around for a few decades; even new teachers have difficulties fully integrating interactive, engaging technology into their daily teaching and learning.

The issue is that most teachers are pretty good with what I will call "easy" technology, such as updating their status on their smartphones. But being good at basic consumer technology does not prepare you for navigating complex, interactive websites (or facilitating your students to do so) or creating engaging, interactive whiteboard lesson plans. These skills must be learned, and it doesn't help that some of the platforms are not all that user-friendly.

Technology is an incredible education multiplier, which is why it is being increasingly integrated into absolutely everything. My advice? Embrace it. Your students do! I'll talk about it more in the lesson-planning chapters.

Don't Get Disillusioned!

Okay... well! This has not been a very motivational chapter, has it? But it's been necessary, I think. My allegiance is to you, the new teacher, and not the system. And you deserve to know everything about teaching, warts and all.

Let's move on!

What Makes a Good Teacher?

What makes a good teacher in the education world?

Teachers who are achieving excellent student results all have a certain blend of traits. These traits, applied in differing proportions depending upon the make-up of the classroom from year to year, describe an elementary teacher who is doing good things for children's education.

Of course, everything in this chapter is all my humble opinion! I certainly expect some disagreement, but I'd like to point out that we are members of a public-service profession with a very high calling - nothing less than the future of civilized society, if you want to get right down to it. (I'm really very humble about our influence, aren't I?) Society has high expectations for elementary school teachers. But then, so do we, when our own children start going to school!

To bring this discussion down from my lofty ideals to reality, when it comes right down to it, what makes a good teacher is defined by what's good for kids.

How do you know if you are suited to becoming an elementary teacher? Well... you just know! It usually boils down to one realization: You love to work with kids. You'd rather become a teacher than do anything else because working around children energizes you rather than wears you out.

But teaching is not just "being around kids" - that's babysitting or being a nanny (both of which require their own set of skills for success). If you've passed the first self-test of loving being in the presence of children every day, you need to move to the second step in self-assessment: What exactly do you like about your relationship with kids? If you are interested in becoming an elementary teacher, this is a very important question. Let's look at some effective teacher traits to help answer it.

Traits of Effective Teachers

Are good teachers born with certain "super teacher" characteristics? Do teacher instincts have to come naturally? Absolutely not. Every one of these characteristics can be learned through experience and self-reflection. Whether they come naturally or through life experience, the great teachers - the ones you want to emulate - have the following qualities.

A Sense of Purpose

Why are you here?

There are many, many people - even well-paid professionals - who hold jobs for the sole purpose of making money.

Teaching is not one of those jobs. There is too much at stake. You are privileged to hold a job that directly impacts another human being's life during their most influential and formative years. You do remember the names of all your elementary school teachers, don't you?

Putting Kids First

For whom are you here? For yourself or for the kids?

I've known teachers who use the students in their classroom to fulfill their own emotional needs for attention. In short, they want the kids to like them more than they want the kids to learn from them. Buying attention with constant treats or shunning all exercise of authority are two symptoms.

Again, you are here for the kids, not yourself. Period.

Willingness to Take a Stand on Behalf Of Children

This really applies when you are fighting for the education of an individual child, such as a student who is being denied special services due to slowness in the qualification process.

Sense of Humor

Humor is a universal language that can create solid teacher and student relationships. Look for and appreciate the silliness of kids and the situations they get themselves into, and laugh along with them. Infuse your teaching with humor to maintain their attention. A good sense of humor can make a huge difference in your enjoyment of your job, and sometimes it's the only thing that will get a teacher through a tough day.

Advanced practitioners of the art of humor will also have no fear of the ridiculous and will feel free to be silly in front of the kids, willing to act out roles for social studies, or do funny voices during teacher read-alouds. More on that later!

Teaching All Curricula

Once you graduate from college with your elementary education diploma, you are certified to teach it all. So here's the thing: If you have a weak spot when it comes to teaching an area of curriculum, so will your kids. And they'll be set back. And that's not okay because it's *really* hard for them to catch up.

You will find that some teachers don't teach everything required by the state for their grade level. These teachers favor subjects they like to teach and give less attention to other subjects. For example, some elementary teachers love to teach reading and social studies and are uncomfortable with teaching math and science. This usually means that, by the end of the school year, their students have not completed all math and science units... and you can't learn long division in fifth grade if you never mastered subtraction in third grade.

It will not always be easy to keep up with the year-long plan, believe me. Which brings me to the next item...

Planning

There is only one way to teach everything that must be taught - planning. Planning is a critical element of teacher success. If lesson planning doesn't come naturally to you, never fear: I cover it in depth in a later chapter.

Organization

Organization goes hand-in-hand with planning. Even with a great plan, you'll need an organized room - a place where you and your students can experience an uncluttered learning environment and can find the things needed for learning quickly and easily.

Tip: The dollar store is an organized teacher's best friend!

Collaboration

Today's elementary classroom teacher is expected to be an active partner in grade-level and grade-band planning and brainstorming. Bring good questions and ideas to the table and follow through on your promises; these are the best ways to bring out the collaborative nature in other teachers.

Creativity

No matter how cut-and-dried a curriculum may be, there is always room for a teacher to add some personal flair. Use your creativity to serve the education process, not as an end in itself. Great teachers don't cut out snowflakes simply for the sake of making something pretty to hang in the classroom, but they *do* cut them out to examine crystal patterns after capturing real snowflakes on black paper outside (also, they just happen to make really pretty decorations to hang in the classroom!).

Tip: Pinterest is a creative teacher's best friend!

Endless Patience

Never forget how you were at their age. Maybe you were shy, slow to read, socially awkward, or obnoxious. No matter what kind of kid you were, there is no doubt that you weren't exactly like everyone else at your age, and you probably weren't always a joy for adults to be around.

But you also know that you needed teacher influence in your life, even if you resented it or didn't appreciate it at the time. Now you are *that* teacher, and each and every kid needs you, whether they realize it or not.

Teaching is the Future of Everything

And you are the future of teaching! I really mean that. You are setting out on a wonderful journey, and I'm going to do everything I can to help you along the way.

Your First Classroom Experiences

Are you are already done with your student-teaching practicum? Please don't skip ahead! This one chapter is focused mainly on our pre-service college students, but I think it is important to fully understand their situation (even if you only recently completed this phase) so we can reach out to them and proactively assist, even if they don't ask.

~

Every education program includes a period of time for real-world application of what you are learning in the college classroom. This student-teaching period (or practicum), is one of the best parts of getting an education degree. Most non-teaching degree programs don't include any time at all in a practical work environment, so student-teaching is a great bonus. I personally think that college students should spend *much* more time in the classroom, but the time that is allowed (which varies by program) can really help launch you quickly into your first year of successful teaching if approached correctly.

As with most things in life, it comes down to your attitude. I see many, many pre-service teachers who regard their practicum as another university class to get through so they can check it off on their path toward graduation (yes, I've read what you post on your public social media!). Well, let me tell you: the path to being an outstanding teacher begins during your practicum. During this time you will learn critical skills regarding interacting with both children and other teachers - but only if you make that your primary goal.

There is a huge variety of approaches that different universities take to student-teaching programs. In general, however, there will usually be an initial exposure to teaching, characterized by observations and short-term interactions in various classrooms and grade levels. Then, eventually, you will be expected to fully take on a classroom for a certain period of time.

In this chapter, I'll be giving you some general pointers about taking control of your own student-teaching destiny. These pointers will apply most directly to your initial, observational exposure to real-world schools, but they will set the stage for your later, full-time interactions with students in their natural environment. When we get into Part Two, I will provide a lot more tips on how to take over and successfully manage when you are completely in charge.

Are you ready to set foot into your first elementary school for your practicum? Let's get started!

Student-Teacher Professionalism

I put this item first - even before the steps to effective learning - because it is critically important. School staff members will apply a tentative label to you the first time they glance in your direction; they are only human, and this is what humans do. But you know what? So will the students.

Remember, to young children, you are not a college student – you are an adult authority figure who is at nearly the same level in their minds as their teacher. Don't do anything that will diminish this. And that begins with your appearance, which boils down to the clothes and makeup that you choose to wear. Figure out quickly how the regular teachers in the building dress and strive to do the same.

Second, before you walk into the school building, turn the volume off on your cell phone and put it in your bag. I have seen student-teachers checking their phones and texting in the back of the classroom as if they were sitting in a lecture hall. I don't think I need to tell you why this is a very bad idea that is not well-received by classroom teachers.

Third, it's time to be on your best behavior. This is akin to being a member of the wedding party on your sister's big day. You are not the center of attention, but you're pretty close to it, and you have to smile and be gracious and keep up appearances for the entire length of the event. This will be good practice for staying "in character" for six hours a day in front of your students when you take over your initial classroom.

Building Your Own Program

No matter what program your university has laid out for you to complete, I highly suggest that you establish your own agenda, as well. If this dovetails with your college course expectations, great. The main point here is to not miss any opportunities for learning and growth. Here are the three basic steps to success:

Observe

In short, be a sponge. There is no detail that is too small for you to notice inside or outside your assigned classroom. It will be easy to notice the big things, such as student behavior episodes or the main points presented on the interactive whiteboard during the lesson. But the real value is often in the details. I encourage you to imagine that you are a "classroom anthropologist" who is carefully searching for patterns in a small, closed society... and the patterns that are often of greatest importance are taking place around the edges.

What I mean is, don't be so distracted by what's going on at center stage that you're missing what's going on outside the spotlight. For example:

- During the presentation of a lesson, what are the kids on the fringes doing?

- If children are asked to partner up and discuss, how does the partnering happen?

- What's going on in the groups that seem to be unfocused or unresponsive?

- What little classroom routines can you observe that are occurring even without teacher direction?

- Why do some kids transition quickly between subjects and others do not?

Be observant of every detail in the classroom, and keep a particular lookout for those children who are not naturally engaging with adults and easy to interact with. These are the kids whom you will need to become an expert at engaging when you go full-time, so you need to understand how and why they are on the periphery rather than in the middle of the action. They are not necessarily hard to *teach*, but they can be hard to *reach*, and your observations will pay dividends in the future if you understand them at a deeper level.

Take Notes

Do not skip this step. Get a composition notebook or a spiral-bound notebook and keep a journal. It will have to be handwritten (you can't be typing in the back of the classroom or distracting students), but you will want to capture your thoughts and insights about what you are seeing. Plus, having something handy to write on will allow you to capture questions to be answered later... and questions are the key to rapid learning.

Ask Questions

There are two types of questions to be asked. First, there are questions that you ask of yourself as you observe. For example, "Why is this happening?"

Asking this type of question will help you get to the root cause of classroom behavior issues, learning engagement problems, or social interactions between the children. It will also help you understand how an effective classroom teacher is achieving a certain result. When you ask yourself "how" and "why," you begin to notice nuances such as tone of voice, silence, or even more subtle things, like meaningful looks and other nonverbal communication.

The second type of questions are those that you ask the teacher whom you are observing. In general, they will take the form of, "Why did you do it this way?" I can't emphasize the importance of this enough; in a few seconds, you can get the distilled knowledge of years of teaching - but only if you ask. An experienced classroom teacher may have learned something so long ago that she now does it naturally; she'll think to reveal the reasoning behind it only if you ask.

A word to the wise: If you observe a teacher who is having a very difficult time with behavior or lesson delivery, be judicious about the questions you ask, particularly if you see that the teacher (who is only human) is having a difficult time emotionally with it. Questions can usually be asked later, just not in the immediate aftermath of an event.

Now let's talk about the types of teachers you may encounter when you start spending time at school.

A Realistic Look at Mentors

Here's a good question: why does a classroom teacher want to work with a college student? I mean, what's in it for them? This, of course, relates very closely to another question: what kind of mentor teacher will you get?

I believe very strongly in providing total honesty to the people who read and follow Classroom Caboodle. I'm all about your success, and that means I must reveal to you a secret. Here it is: *Not all people are the same.* Earthshaking, right? Not really, of course, but the point is that building up false expectations about who or what your mentor teacher will be can lead to some disappointment. As much as we would like to think that every teacher can be a perfect mentor for us during our developmental period, this simply cannot be true. Teachers are human and come in all varieties.

Hosting an untested college student can be a major undertaking and (once you begin your take-over-the-classroom phase) a very big classroom disruption. Since you are such an unknown quantity from the teacher's perspective, why are any of them willing to risk it?

Here's why:

- A teacher may want to give back to the profession and inspire a new generation that can positively influence children. Congratulations! You won the mentor-teacher lottery!

- A teacher may want to have another set of hands in a difficult room, such as a combination room with two grade levels. This means lots of work for you, but the chance for some really great – if challenging – on-the-job training.

- A teacher may want long lunches and frequent out-of-classroom breaks during the day. Yes, these teachers exist, and you know it's true because you had some of them when you were in elementary school. For all their trouble in mentoring you, they can look forward to a month or more of doing virtually nothing and still getting paid. Their level of abandonment of their student-teachers will vary.

This is all to say that I encourage you to go in without preconceived notions. Look for the positive and be ready to handle the negative… all the while knowing that even if your practicum does not fit the image you have in your mind, you will still learn a whole lot from your first time in the classroom.

Your Very First "Interview"

How do successful job-hunters act during teacher interviews? Well, let's see...

- They dress professionally.

- They are interested in everything going on at their target school.

- They showcase their commitment to educating children.

- They ask intelligent questions.

Hmmm... that sounds an awful lot like the things a successful student-teacher does!

If you are planning to seek a job in the district where you are doing your practicum, then you must treat every single moment that you are on school property as an interview situation. More than one student-teacher has found a position in this way. Principals are like any bosses; they would rather go with a known quantity if they have the choice. If you are that known quantity (known for your excellence, that is), then you may have an edge in an interview.

Even if you aren't seeking a job in your practicum district, you'd be surprised at who knows who in the education world; many back-channel discussions take place between educators during hiring season. Also, you really do need great letters of recommendation, not only from your mentor-teacher, but also from the principal at the school.

And even if those two arguments don't convince you, believe me, you can obtain a heck of a lot of experiences during your student-teaching time that will allow you to discuss excellent real-world examples when you're answering questions during interviews.

In short, the wise student-teacher will treat her practicum with all the seriousness of a teacher interview.

Getting Sick, Staying Well

Health may be the last thing on your mind when you begin your student-teaching, but please give these concerns your full attention. Schools are miniature melting pots that draw in all kinds of germs, then provide ideal incubating conditions: crowded classrooms, packed coat closets, and the active germ-spreading habits of children.

Believe me, you would be shocked at what children will put into their mouths... and then remove and leave on desks for unsuspecting teachers to pick up!

I spent the first several years of teaching being constantly sick until I built up an immunity to every possible germ combination. My story is not unique among new teachers. When you combine this with the additional stress of going to college and teaching at the same time (plus a few of those late nights you might be indulging in), you have a perfect scenario for getting really sick. At a minimum, expect a few sniffles, but please do everything in your power to cut your risks:

- Lots and lots of hand-washing
- Hand sanitizer in between hand-washings
- Being cautious of horizontal surfaces!

If it's a flat surface, it is essentially a petri dish where it is inadvisable to set anything that is going to come anywhere close to your mouth.

Stay healthy; stay happy.

Social Media And Your Paparazzi

The time to lock down your social media profiles is before you head into your practicum experience. Kids are inquisitive, and they will search you out online like rabid fans. Their parents may go fishing for information, as well, once they learn your name.

Make certain any social media account that has your real name and/or picture can only be viewed by those to whom you grant permission. If you have accounts for which this is not an option, then be certain that your user name and image cannot be easily traced to you.

Like it or not, you are becoming a role model for children. It is quite likely that there are things in your online ramblings that are quite relevant to your college experience and yet highly inappropriate for impressionable young children. You know exactly what I mean - again, I have read a fair number of your public social media posts!

And just to be clear: it is not okay to interact socially with your elementary students online. That brings with it so many red flags, it is not even worth considering.

~

So... you now know how to make the most of your practicum. It's time to start covering topics that apply in some measure to all teachers, whether they are still in college or have made it through the job search and are looking forward to their very own classroom.

PART 2

Building a Community of Learners

All children want to belong to a community. Great teachers build communities that are accepting of all.

~ *Betsy Weigle*

Taking Center Stage

Sooner or later, it will happen: you will find yourself standing in front of a classroom filled with children. It may be for a lesson or a read-aloud, or it may be simply to introduce yourself. Regardless of the purpose, you will find yourself asking the age-old question that all teachers have pondered:

"How in the world do I get them to pay attention?!"

You can find all kinds of tips and tricks about how to get kids to settle down in the classroom. I'll even cover some in later chapters. But understand one thing very clearly: there is no trick or technique that is going to cause your students to *want* to engage in what you are saying. Techniques are helpful as quick reminders or to direct attention, but true "eyes-on-the-teacher" engagement comes from giving the kids someone to be interested in. And that someone is you.

The way you conduct yourself in the classroom – the way you speak, the way you pause, the way you smile, the way you walk around, *everything you do* – will either cause children to listen or cause them to turn away and find something else to pay attention to.

When you understand the rules of naturally holding the attention of children, you will find that getting them to engage in anything becomes extremely easy. But, if you do not learn these fundamental rules of attention, you will struggle with every aspect of your teaching: classroom management will be difficult; delivering lessons will be tiresome; your days will be one non-stop attempt to get kids to listen to you.

It doesn't have to be that way. Let's start with some background principles.

Holding Children's Attention

I say this over and over again on my website: children are simply small humans. They lack maturity and experience, but they are subject to the same basic instincts as adults. This means that they much prefer to be around interesting people than boring people.

Do you like to be around boring people? Do you like to go on dates or sit in meetings and listen to somebody drone on? Of course not! It is human nature to be fascinated by interesting people - that's exactly what drives the popularity of celebrity gossip. And you're in luck! You will not have to engage in celebrity antics to gain attention from elementary children. But you will have to embrace your role as a *classroom* celebrity.

You see, elementary school children want to love their teacher. They want their teacher to be a little bit larger than life, someone they can look up to and respect and emulate. This role has already been created for you, and all you must do is step into it and claim it.

If you don't claim the role of "most interesting person in your classroom," then believe me, your students will find someone else to pay attention to. And that you *cannot* have if you want to positively influence your kids through classroom management and instruction.

Every Classroom is a Stage

"But," you protest, "I'm not an interesting person! I'm not outgoing, even among my own friends, let alone in a classroom filled with children."

Good news for you: you don't have to be a natural at this - you can develop that over time; even experienced teachers act differently in the classroom than they do around their families and friends. And you have one advantage that most actors don't: you don't have to worry about having a tough audience. These are, after all, small children, and they are not very critical of teachers who may be acting a little bit. In fact, they are extremely accepting and supportive if you give them a reason to be.

Given the information in this chapter, you will know exactly how to become an interesting person in the eyes of your students. And that's all that counts.

Becoming a Super-interesting Person

You may think that being interesting comes down only to what you say when you are speaking to your group. Nope. It's the whole package:

- How you speak (not just what you say)
- How you dress
- How you wear your hair and makeup
- How you smile
- What you eat for lunch
- The kind of coffees you drink

... and on and on. Your students will be scrutinizing absolutely everything about you every moment of the day. You can do something as simple as wearing a new tie or scarf and score interest points without saying a single thing. What you say when you *do* speak is icing on the cake, which confirms that you are a fascinating person who will be discussed by all of your students every single night:

"Mom, guess what Ms. Smith did today?!"

So, how do you take advantage of this? Easy: be yourself! As long as you are within the bounds of appropriate behavior, don't fear being different from other teachers - your kids will love you for it because they will feel different (superior) by association. Strive to be the unique person that only *you* can be... but with a slight amount of exaggeration, like a stage actor who is a bit larger than life so the people in the back row can appreciate the character she is playing.

And change it up - often. Keep them wondering, "What will she do next?" This is not faking it. This is stepping up, into the shoes of great teachers. You will still be "you," but with special sauce added.

You can even conduct some interesting experiments. Dress blandly for a week, then dress to stand out. How do the kids react? Do a non-animated read-aloud, then one with all the drama you can muster, including outrageous character voices. You'll see how "flair" can increase learning in children.

What's next? Well, even though you want to stand out as unique, you also need to give your students multiple points of connection so they can think to themselves:

"Wow, I'm a little bit like Ms. Smith!"

And for that, we need to have a discussion about sharing personal information.

Your Public Profile

It's only natural for your students to want to know more about their favorite teacher. But where's the line - and how do you avoid crossing it?

My students have always ended up knowing the names of my children, my pets, and some of my favorite things. I, personally, have found that my willingness to share these personal tidbits helps them buy into me as their teacher and classroom leader more quickly.

I raised this issue with my followers, and here are some of the excellent comments provided by your fellow teachers:

> Amy: "I absolutely believe in making a personal connection with students by letting them know who you are. My students not only know my family members' names, but they get to meet them during the school year. They also know my favorite foods, holiday, etc."

> Cynthia: "The other day, one of my students asked if my daughter knew how many of her stories I shared with them! My students become my kids. It makes me more approachable if they know something about my

life. It also means they are more willing to share their life stories with me (and some of them really need to)."

Sarah: "It's important that kids get to know you so they realize you are a real person and not just some woman who lives at school." (I love this one!)

KayLynn: "I did have a student who once thought the staff room must have bunk-beds in it for all of us live-at-school teachers! I think students feel a deeper connection with their teacher if they know more about them. It also makes your classroom feel homier!"

Erin: "Showing them that we're real people outside of school helps them to see what's important to us. They're always interested in what I wear, how I do my nails and makeup, and how I'm doing in bowling."

Colene: "They want to know that you are someone who cares about them and their education – in other words, they want to know if they can trust you. It also helps them bond with you as their mentor."

Jennifer: "I always share some things about my family life. My first graders are always so excited to see my daughter or son somewhere and call them by name. It sure surprises my own children!"

Tracie: "Building trust is SO important in a teacher/student relationship! It always warms my heart when my students mistakenly call me 'Mom.'"

Tips for Personal Sharing

If you are not a naturally outgoing person, you may wonder where to begin. As I mentioned before, your devoted followers (your students) are a pretty forgiving audience! They don't need a ton of details about your life, just enough to give them something to giggle about and tell their parents when they get home from school.

Guidelines for Sharing

Don't make it all about you; provide snippets of your life as you invite them to share about theirs.

Bring pictures of your family at the beginning of the year. Bonus points for pet pictures! Kids LOVE to know about your furry friends. Don't have a cat or dog? Get a goldfish and give it a funny name. Still too much commitment? Go to the pet store and buy a cricket or capture a beetle and keep it in a shoebox. Talking about *any* pet will score huge points with your kids. I can hear the after-school conversation now:

> "Oh my gosh, Mom! Did you know that Ms. Smith has a pet beetle?!"

Set guidelines for what is appropriate for them to know and let them know gently when they have gone too far in their questioning. What's generally okay?

- Family member names and ages
- Favorite things
- What you did over the weekend/summer vacation
- What inspires you

Generally, you can share with your kids the same things you'd share with a casual acquaintance - in other words, strictly "safe-for-work" details.

And a final idea: Bring your family members to class if you can, if only for a short Q&A session. But they need to be ready to be treated like rock stars!

A Community Built On Sharing

Why is the sharing of personal details so powerful? It comes down to basic human nature: we share personal details with people who matter to us - with people with whom we feel a connection. "Feeling a connection" is exactly what you want your classroom community to be based upon. When we allow others into our personal lives – even a tiny bit – then we are being a little vulnerable to them, and this naturally earns their trust.

Enter the "Drama Queen"

So far we've talked about letting your unique personality shine and sharing some selected information in order to connect with your children. Now let's talk about taking it to the next level. Every successful teacher of elementary children will tell you that a bit of drama is critical for catching and maintaining children's attention. Just as you are going to slightly accentuate your unique qualities, like that stage actor I mentioned earlier, you are also going to accentuate the way you make your points.

How? Consider a new-teacher question that I presented to my followers for input:

> "I'm a new teacher and still suffering from a problem I had as a student-teacher. I'm not naturally a dramatic person, or even an outspoken one. My kids seem to stop paying attention to me so easily, even during a read-aloud. Their attention drifts, and then the

behavior begins. I feel self-conscious if I go 'over the top' when teaching, but I've seen other teachers who are this way in front of students and seem to hold attention better.

"I'm struggling with how to be this kind of teacher. Any ideas?"

Can you relate? Let's see what experienced teachers had to say about adding some attention-getting drama:

Anna: "Pick up your cell and do a fake call to a parent in front of the class, going over the top about how great 'Jessica' is performing!"

Sebastion: "Get really silly every once in a while: do a Native American dance during social studies or act like a robot during science. The kids will never know what's next!"

Cole: "Sometimes a well-placed whisper will add to the suspense. Use it sparingly but at least once a day to make a point."

Ellen: "Practice your read-alouds before doing them for your class. Where will you dramatically pause and ask, 'What do you think happens next?' How will your character voices sound? Where will you stop reading to keep them guessing until the next day?"

Sarah: "Having trouble acting in a way that doesn't feel natural? Then use some props. Kids love the unexpected. If you are teaching a lesson with a baseball theme, then put on a baseball hat and a jersey, for example. It helps you play a role more naturally, as if you are actually a different person. And speaking of props, have a few funny ones in your room. I use to have a soft foam ball that had a pattern of an eye. If someone was acting up a bit, I'd position it on the filing cabinet so it was 'looking' at them and say, 'I've got my eye on you.'"

Do you see the common theme? Acting. If your students' attention is wandering, you are going to have to up your crazy-meter a bit. It won't feel natural at first, but within a day or two, you'll be pulling it off with ease. The kids will love it and will end up learning in spite of themselves.

You Decide The Role You Will Play

So what happens when we put it all together? Well, look at it from the students' perspective by imagining two student-teacher scenarios (you can easily apply this to first-year teachers, too):

Picture a student-teacher entering a school building. She is well-prepared for the requirements she must meet in order to get credits, but hesitant to go beyond them, and it shows. She enters the room quietly and slips to her out-of-the-way spot with hardly a word of greeting. During instruction, she hangs to the side of the class, doesn't engage unless someone speaks to her, and, when she does teach, she appears subdued... not surprising since she's obviously a little nervous.

Next, picture the same teacher walking into the classroom - still nervous, but putting on a brave smile and faking it to overcome her racing heart. She's wearing a basic outfit, but she's added a scarf for some visual interest. Instead of heading to the back of the classroom to find a safe spot, she mingles with the kids a bit as they are getting settled, engaging in short snippets of conversation about what they did the night before. During independent work, she doesn't just observe;

she circulates and challenges the kids to explain their thinking. When she's doing a read-aloud, she uses a few dramatic pauses and some funny voices. In short, she's not taking over the classroom or trying to outshine her mentor teacher... she's simply being an interesting person.

Now imagine that you are an elementary-aged child. Which one do you want your teacher to be? The instinctive reaction of any child will be to pay more attention to and engage more with the second teacher. They can't help it - it is built-in to their very nature to be more attracted to an interesting person who shows interest in them.

Be that person. For the sake of your classroom management, student engagement, and success at teaching children, be that person during both your practicum *and* when you take over your first classroom.

Creating Teacher/Student Relationships

The last chapter was all about how you present yourself, with a few tips thrown in about interacting verbally with children. Now we are going to dive deeply into that teacher-to-student interaction. Once you've gotten yourself noticed by being a uniquely interesting version of yourself, it's time to build on that relationship.

And you should have no doubt about this: you must have a relationship with a child in order to get them to do anything, from paying attention to mastering their multiplication facts.

Think about that: whom would you want to learn from - somebody who shows interest in your progress, or somebody who treats you as just another data point? You know the answer... and you know that your students will find much greater success if they believe that their teacher cares deeply about them. And not only cares, but interacts at a level that they can feel in their bones is genuine.

At some point in their lives - hopefully - your students will decide to learn things because they want to know more. But in elementary school, most of your students will learn things because they want to please their favorite teacher (that's you!). Building relationships will dramatically increase your ability to exercise effective classroom management, and from that will grow your ability to engage with and instruct children to their highest potential.

So how do we build teacher-student relationships? The same way we build *all* relationships: we talk, and we listen. Of course, we talk and listen with *intention* so that we move the process along as quickly as possible.

Let's get started. We are going to be covering things that apply to both student-teachers and new teachers during their first full-time classroom jobs.

Showing Interest

How interested are you in princesses? Do you find lizard facts to be fascinating? How about other people's pets - do you love to hear details about their antics? Well, I don't know about you, but I can generally do without princess, lizard, or pet knowledge. However, I am *very* interested in my students, which means that what's important to them becomes important to me.

When I was a student-teacher, my mentor teacher felt that a personal relationship was so critical with her students that she kept a checklist of all their names. She literally checked off each kid to ensure that she had a one-on-one, personal conversation with all of them every single week. She did this the first few weeks of school to ensure that nobody was left out, and after that, it became habitual. I have always remembered her level of dedication. I think of how I would have felt showing up at school and having a trusted adult – an authority figure, no less – take the time every few days to talk to me about whatever was important to me. How would that make you feel?

Well, I don't know about you, but even as an adult, that sort of attention makes me feel great! Think of how it makes a child feel.

So, yes, take notes if you need to, but learn and remember what your children are interested in. Learn the names of their siblings and their pets. Remember when they mention that they go to their grandma's house on Saturday so you can ask about it on Monday. And on and on... great teacher-student relationships are built upon these small details.

You don't have to have in-depth discussions about anything; a meaningful discussion with a student can literally take thirty seconds. There are all kinds of times during the day when you can find thirty seconds:

- Before the bell rings out on the blacktop in the morning
- During transitions between subjects
- In the lunch line

A quick remark about a student's choice of shoes or their new hat is easy to make. Asking if their family finally made the decision about where to spend Christmas takes ten seconds. You just have to show that you notice and that you remember what's important to them.

There's no pandering involved; we're not begging them to pay attention to us. We are simply treating them as individuals who are worthy of our time and thoughts.

And remember: you are not competing with them! There is no need to one-up them with a little bragging. If you share thoughts from your own life, then present then in a way that furthers the relationship. After you share a quick detail or story, you'll want the student to be thinking:

"Wow! Ms. Adams is kind of like me!"

Not:

"Ms. Adams always seems to have a better story than I do."

Stay focused on the goal.

Leveling the Playing Field

When it comes to showing interest in children, it's very important to be certain that the physical layout and the functioning of your classroom does not favor any child over another. Obviously, there will always be "front" and "not-in-front" parts to your classroom. Make sure you rotate the children through all sections.

And never, ever locate students in your room so that it is more convenient for you. For example, it is all too common for teachers to place those kids with IEP's, who must leave the room for Special Education support, near the door. The justification is that they are then able to slip in and out without bothering the rest of the students.

That is just plain awful. When somebody steps into your room, they should not be able to tell who your Special Education students are. They must be fully integrated with the other students. How they enter and leave the classroom is only a matter of setting expectations. By the way, when they do return from being away from your close-knit group, they should be greeted with, "Welcome back; here's what we're doing." Treating Special Education kids in any way that diminishes them can really get my temper up!

But this principle doesn't apply only to kids with IEP's; trouble-prone, talkative, or even checked-out students belong at the front of the room just as much as tuned-in, behaving kids.

Student-centered teaching means that every child in our rooms feels very keenly that they are not a second-class citizen in any way. Maybe they get treated that way in other areas of their lives, but not while they are under our care.

No Labels!

Humans love to label other humans. Unfortunately, this labeling usually occurs almost immediately after being introduced! And, of course, humans are also extremely reluctant to change labels once they have been applied. Are you still trying to escape some labels that your family applied to you in your youth? Yeah… I thought so.

Just as we will never allow children to diminish each other by labeling (covered in more detail later), we should never do it ourselves. And this applies to both "good" and "bad" labels. It's as detrimental to call undue attention to your high-performing students as it is to single out those who are having difficulty.

This is what I had to say on this topic in my book *Elementary Einsteins: 4 Simple Steps to Challenging Gifted Students in Your Classroom:*

I truly believe that every child is gifted at something, and each and every one of those gifts needs to be recognized and celebrated in the elementary classroom. That's how we build community.

"Specialness" is often a label that is used to set people apart. This will unravel your classroom community very quickly. As a consequence, I do not even use the term "gifted" when referring to the gifted kids in my room. It's very similar to the way I do not use the term "Special Education" when referring to kids with IEP's.

Instead, I establish an expectation that every child gets the individual attention they need to succeed. This allows me to describe each child's needs in terms of what they *individually require for effective learning.*

Then, when other students learn that certain kids are going to a gifted program, I explain that those children have a different learning style; they need to have some project-based learning, which is why they leave the classroom one day a week to receive it. In the same vein, I explain that Special Education kids need more one-on-one and small-group support, and that's why they receive extra help or pull-out time.

When every child in your room knows deep in his heart that he will receive exactly what he needs from his teacher to learn most effectively, he won't begrudge the time or attention other kids get. In this way, everyone is "special"... but no one is any more special than anyone else.

Praising Children

Recently, I heard from a Special Education teacher who was striving to make a real impact on her students. Here's what she asked:

> "So many of my students don't even believe in themselves. They don't even TRY. I can teach the kids phonics and decoding and help improve their reading, but what I really want to instill in them is self-confidence. That's what will take them far in life. If you have any ideas about motivating students to believe in themselves, please share."

Let me share with you what I told her. It all comes down to the fine art of praising children.

Teacher Recognition: The Technique

The first approach is your personal, teacher-to-student way of building up their self-esteem. It includes congratulating them on their smarts, but in a very genuine way. Those little people just want to be appreciated. Correct complimenting is important, because they need to be appreciated for the right things - this is school, after all, and your approach should lead to increased learning.

It's easy to tell a student, "You're so smart," but that's too general. It means a lot more if your expressions are tied to a specific example. The wise teacher avoids empty, generalized, feel-good compliments such as:

> "Wow, you got done quickly!"

Or:

"That's a beautiful picture you drew."

These make the recipient feel good, but not for the right reasons. Keep compliments specific and focus them on children's thinking:

"That's an interesting math strategy. Why did you decide that was the best way?"

Plus, it's much more effective to show kids you think they're smart by expressing surprise at the answer they got, or inferring that they found a solution that even you didn't think of:

"Wow! Look at the picture you drew! Tell me about the colors you chose."

Or:

"I can't believe you diagrammed your answer that way. Impressive! What made you think of it?"

You understand what I mean: we are going for those kinds of reactions that tell kids that you are genuinely surprised and impressed by what they've accomplished. That seems so much more "real" than standard phrases.

Think of how you would like people to react to some accomplishment that you have done (with surprise and admiration), and understand that little children want exactly the same thing.

Peer Recognition: The Biggest Motivator in School

The second approach really adds the "sauce" to instilling self-esteem. And that is building up a child in front of his classmates. This cannot be done in a structured way, by calling a child to the front of the room and giving a little speech on how great he is. That's just embarrassing to him. Again, it must be done as if it's part of your normal flow of teaching.

This is accomplished by saying things such as:

> "Hey, everyone. Listen to what Matthew just came up with. It's an amazing answer. Matthew, could you explain it to the group?"

Or:

> "When I was checking all of your papers from yesterday, I was really impressed with the punctuation that Maria used. Here, I'll put her paper under the document camera so you can all see it."

This doesn't even have to be in front of an entire classroom; any opportunity you can take to build up Matthew or Maria in front of even one other child will do amazing things for their self-esteem.

Matthew will be thinking:

> "Wow, my teacher is so impressed that she wants all these other kids to see what I'm doing so they can learn from me. Maybe I *am* pretty smart..."

Wouldn't you have loved to have felt that way when you were in elementary school? I would have! Complimenting is a fine art and a key skill for any teacher who wants to build a strong student/teacher relationship with a class - the kind of relationship in which the kids want to display the correct behavior just because you ask them, not because they have to.

Read-alouds Begin Relationships

So, where do you begin if you are a student-teacher doing a practicum? Aside from generally being pleasant to be around (as noted previously), your best bet for kick-starting a relationship is a teacher read-aloud. Look for or ask for the opportunity to spend ten minutes reading to the children. Start with a picture-book read-aloud and choose the book wisely, with input from your mentor teacher. Ensure that it is grade-level appropriate, related to lesson content, engaging, and makes kids think and question. Keep it fairly short.

Gather the kids on the floor, with you seated in a chair. Pulling the kids closer increases your control and keeps them from pursuing their own activities at the far corners of the room. Read, pausing to share pictures, and ask simple questions to encourage the students to engage in conversation:

"Why do you think he decided to do that?"

"What do you think will happen next?"

And always follow up with:

"Well, why do you think that?"

Encourage higher-level thinking and compliment the students, as we've already discussed. A read-aloud is as close as you can get to a foolproof relationship starter. Use it!

Managing Your Classroom

Is there any other subject besides classroom management that causes new teachers – and a fair number of experienced teachers – more headaches? Based on my experience, no. Classroom management will make or break your teaching experience.

It doesn't have to be that way. Management is very difficult if you are only relying on a series of tips and tricks to deal with particular situations. It becomes much easier, however, if you understand the philosophy and benefits of forming a close-knit classroom team. Those benefits are so great that I can condense the majority of my classroom management advice into three chapters. I think you'll pick up on the fact that community-building approaches are sprinkled throughout all of my teaching, but the fundamentals are right here.

A Special Note for Teachers on Practicum

If you are starting your first teaching job, then the ideas in this chapter will be immediately applicable to your situation. However, if you are just heading into your student-teaching practicum, you will have very little control over the nature of the classroom community; you have to work with what already exists.

However, there are lots of ideas here that will help you. Yes, you may not be inheriting an ideal situation, but you do have authority and influence over some group dynamics. Also, some of the specific interventions that I go over will be very helpful to you.

The Power of Belonging

What is so great about a team-based approach to classroom management? Well, it helps to think about it from the perspective of a pack. And I mean "pack" as in pack of wolf cubs. I'm serious! The key concept is that the members of your classroom want to belong to a pack, or group. All children desperately want to be part of a group. That desire to be a member of a group will have three very powerful influences on your classroom management:

1. The members of the group will internalize and emulate group norms.

In other words, if you have created a classroom team that is polite and respectful, the members of that team will be much more likely to be polite and respectful in order to remain members in good standing of the group. It is human nature that we conform to the norms established by a group to which we want to belong.

This fact alone will alleviate a lot of your classroom management headaches by diminishing the number of individual behavior problems.

2. The members of the group will enforce the norms of the group.

All people, including children, become uncomfortable with behavior that disrupts a group to which they belong and will often correct their peers for misbehavior. For example, if you have established that one of your group norms is to quietly transition between subjects without talking, then you will hear kids shushing those who feel like chattering - without you needing to say a thing.

That's one small example, but you get the point: the group will work to enforce ideal behavior so as not to "ruin it" for everyone.

3. The members of the group will dislike being separated from the group.

Humans especially like to be part of a group if the group is doing something fun! Picture this: I was teaching a science lesson to a combined classroom (my students plus another class). Kids LOVE science, and this was a very hands-on session, involving experiments in buoyancy with "life boats" (cups of different sizes) loaded with "passengers" (metal washers) and tubs of water.

With over fifty kids, I knew that any misbehavior could get out of hand very quickly, and things could turn messy and unsafe. I set very strong expectations with my class about following proper scientific procedures exactly. Within five minutes, two kids had received their one warning, repeated their offenses, and were on the sidelines, watching and taking notes for five minutes, as other kids got to test how many passengers could be loaded into the boats before sinking.

The rest of the class became model scientists after that; in spite of the temptation to go wild with the materials, they studiously implemented the scientific method and spoke very precisely, asking the right questions and using the proper terms.

The Impact of Separation

And this, ladies and gentlemen, is the key to no-stress classroom behavior management. I will go through the specific steps for this later, but *separation from the group* provides a very effective consequence for those students not following your expectations - without raising your voice, getting stressed out, or employing complicated reward-tracking systems.

Take note: I am *not* talking about kicking children out of your classroom! Many times, the separation will be as little as two feet away from their normal desk position. In fact, it is much more effective for a child to see the group continuing without them for a minute or two (as with my science example above) than to be completely out of sight.

If the group is a place where a child desperately wants to be (and I'll tell you how to make sure it is), then even sitting off to the side of the room for one minute will cause them to alter their behavior quickly, so as not to be an outsider. Likewise, for the rare behavior that does rise to the level of a trip to the principal, it will not be so much the confrontation with administration that provides a consequence, but rather the complete removal from your classroom community for a period of time.

I simply can't stress this enough: a strong classroom community team must be your classroom management foundation.

Leader of the Pack

So, why is a wolf pack an apt analogy? Because every pack has a leader who sets the norms for all the little wolf pups. And guess who the leader of the pack is in your classroom?

This grows out of our previous discussion about being an authority figure simply by being an adult in an elementary school. You must recognize and accept that you are automatically the leader of the pack and the person who gets to establish all behavior expectations.

You are also the person who has the ability to remove a member from the group and to reinstate that member back into the group. When misbehaving children understand this, you can work through all of your behavior management steps with a calm demeanor and without threats.

When the leader of the pack speaks, the wolves listen!

Of course, you are a benevolent leader. In other words, the members of your little pack will love you as their teacher and their leader and will want to maintain the cohesion of the group.

Creating Your Classroom Team

No matter how old we get, we never really escape elementary school.

Remember the trauma of getting picked for teams out on the playground? The desperate hope that you wouldn't be the last, unwanted person? As an adult, you still don't like the feeling that comes from a group of people going out to lunch and not inviting you.

Remember how uncomfortable you were walking into the grade school lunchroom, fervently hoping that you could find a place to sit so you wouldn't look like an unwanted loner? Do you still feel that way when you walk into a cafeteria filled with groups of people talking and laughing? Of course you do. If you end up sitting alone, you might feel that you are being judged as unworthy of companionship.

Knowing that our students feel this very acutely, our goal as team leaders is clear: we want every single child in our classrooms to feel deep down in their heart that we - their favorite teacher - have specifically and enthusiastically chosen them to be on our team.

How would you have felt as a child if, every time you walked into your classroom, your teacher smiled at you and greeted you and made it very clear that she was thrilled that you were present? Well I don't know about you, but it would have made me feel great - like school was my absolute favorite place to go every day because I knew that I belonged. More importantly, I would have idolized the teacher who made me feel that way.

So, the process of forming a close-knit group is not particularly difficult if you understand your objective. It's made even easier by the fact that your students will take their cues from you; they will watch every move you make and listen to everything you say and imitate it. Here are the basic pointers to creating your classroom team - your own little pack of wolves.

Be Polite

"Please" and "thank you" and "excuse me" must be liberally sprinkled throughout your conversations. Remind your children to use them, too. Along with these polite words, practice polite actions, such as not interrupting. (This starts to cross the line a little bit into setting expectations; we'll get into those in more detail in a moment.)

Be Positive

Smile a lot. Even if you're having a down day, act like your classroom is exactly where you want to be. It doesn't hurt anything to let your kids know you are having a tough day... but, at the same time, you should let them know that being with them makes it better.

Notice Every Child

Never underestimate the power of just noticing... the greatest classroom reward for student effort is a teacher who cares. Although you are forming a group, always remember that it is made up of unique little individuals. And these individuals want their teacher to notice things:

- Their new shoes or coat or hairstyle
- That they are finishing a book that is hard for them
- That they remembered to start their sentences with a capital letter

They even want you to notice when they remember to be polite!

In short, they want to know that their leader cares enough about them to notice things. Noticing doesn't mean making a big deal; pointing to some new shoes and giving a thumbs-up or tapping on a properly punctuated sentence and winking is every bit as effective as saying something.

Allow Nobody to be Diminished in Any Way

Just as teachers should never use public shaming as a behavior management tool, you should never allow children to diminish each other. This is poison to your group. To have children feel unsafe in any way within your classroom (physically or emotionally) will eventually cause them to withdraw from wanting to belong. No labeling allowed by anyone!

Apologies are also important, and we'll talk about them in a minute.

~

Even if you are on your practicum and thus inheriting the team formed by the classroom teacher, you can still start forming your *own* pack the moment you walk into the room. Like I said before, you simply start the process of picking children to belong on your team. Picking them just means following these common-sense steps to let them know you want to be associated with them.

It's not a competition with your mentor teacher; unlike playground games, kids can belong to more than one team at a time!

All About Expectations

You've created a close-knit, respectful, and polite classroom team. An excellent start! But there's more work to do - much more - in order to appropriately handle the student behavior (and misbehavior) you are soon to encounter.

Setting Expectations

Building a strong team is the foundation, but the rest of the house is built with expectations. There is an awful lot that can be said about how to set expectations, but we will keep this discussion down to the basics.

You'll find yourself setting group expectations much more often than setting individual expectations. In general, you will set expectations for the group, then remind individuals about following them. So, let's work our way through a detailed session of setting expectations. This is the kind of session you might experience during the first couple of weeks of school when you are establishing new procedures.

Please don't think that these are only for new teachers kicking off a school year; these are also the types of expectation-setting sessions that you will undertake (for example) when your students are itching to get their hands on the new stream-table science kits! Dirt, water, mess... everything that kids love to play around with! Believe me, explicit expectations are critical to the success of a lesson like that. Let's look at a real-world example to understand how the step-by-step procedure looks and sounds. I received this question through my website contact form:

> "What is the most effective way to distribute equipment in a K-6 fitness class? I need an efficient plan to hand out equipment quickly and efficiently to all students."

Ah... a perfect scenario for our purposes: eager kids who are in the mood to play, being handed stuff to play with. Teachers set student expectations all day long for all manner of tasks, but when we are talking about objects that can be quite tempting to throw/roll/lob at other kids, the stakes are higher. But the same level of temptation could apply to so many things; just replace basketballs with:

- Markers
- iPads
- Lockers
- Band instruments
- Bathroom soap dispensers

Therefore, setting classroom expectations for handling "stuff" takes a different kind of reinforcement than setting expectations for turning in papers or being quiet during a teacher read-aloud. But, if you know how to implement the process below, you'll easily be able to adapt it to less-problematic scenarios.

Don't think that this process is a short and simple recipe, some magic approach that engenders perfect discipline the first time. Nope. This takes time and repetition, but only upfront; after student expectations are set and habits are built, you earn back the time you initially invest.

Let's get started.

Step 1. Arrange the Items Logically

If the situation calls for it, put some thought into accessibility for the item(s) in question. In our fitness class example, that might mean lining up the balls on a bench before class. In your classroom, it could mean placing the clipboards in a bin by the whiteboard.

Remember, the kids themselves will have to get the items in question, so put yourself in their place (actually walk through the process) and figure out how to arrange things in order to avoid pushing and shoving, which leads me to the next step.

Step 2. Consider the Flow

Do the students come up all at the same time? By two's or three's? In a single-file line? Ensure that your arrangement of items coordinates with the preferred process for getting them.

Step 3. Determine Your Student Expectations

Base this upon your experience with the item in question... or grab a clipboard, ball, or jump-rope and see how much trouble you can get into with it! Jot down a few notes if needed, so you don't forget something. Now you are ready for the students.

Step 4. Overview the Item and its Use and Care

Don't be afraid of humor! Give the item a name, call it your friend, say what makes your friend happy or unhappy... use your imagination. Make it brief, but cover all the bases on:

- What it is
- How it is used
- Why it is used
- What constitutes abuse

This is expectation-setting. Use the phrase, "My expectation is..." a few times so you can refer back to it (see step 8).

Step 5. Model the Entire Process

Don't just talk through the process - show them. Walk the path that they will walk, pick it up the way they should pick it up, use it in the correct manner, then put it away properly. Humans are visual learners, and many elementary students cannot easily translate verbal instructions to personal actions. Show them, and they are much more likely to get it.

Tip: How to hold something and walk with it can be a big deal when it comes to laptops or tablets, when dropping equals breaking.

Step 6. Model with a Few Assistants

Draft a few kids from the class to go through the same process you just completed. This time, you will be watching and gently correcting if (when!) they make mistakes.

Step 7. Guide the Class through the Process

Remind them of each step, from the initial line-up to where they will ultimately end up.

Step 8. Stop... Go Back... Repeat

If it is not going well, start over. And I mean from the beginning. Put the stuff away, sit back down, remind them, and do it all over again. Never let students practice a process wrong. If you do, you'll never get the performance you are hoping for. As stated above, invest the time now for dividends that last the entire year.

In extreme circumstances, you may spend the entire time you have allotted for your lesson practicing - or it may just seem like you did! And that's okay... sometimes we just have to out-wait the naughties.

Be open to altering the process; students may have ideas for shaving seconds off a routine once they understand the goal.

~

That's the full process. Apply it in varying measures to every expectation you set. Not everything may require all eight steps, but many things will. If things start to slip over time: repeat, repeat, repeat. Any time expectations are not being met, take the entire class through the process again. You'll find yourself saying the same phrase many times throughout the school year:

"My expectation is that you will..."

Keep that sense of humor! Patience is your best ally when setting expectations.

More Expectations

The situations in which expectations must be established are too numerous to list in detail, but some activities from a typical day will give you an idea of what's involved. This is just a small taste of the comprehensive web of expectations I weave to maintain order:

- How to walk into the building
- How to store coats and backpacks
- How to get chairs down from desks
- How to check in on the interactive whiteboard
- How to hand in homework
- How to work on and turn in the entry task (bell work)

That covers about the first fifteen minutes of the day, and you can already see the premium I place on setting expectations! The expectations for every one of these activities were explained in detail and modeled more than once so that there would be no questions at all about how to do them properly.

I could sum it up by saying that the list of activities the kids do *without* an expectation-setting session would have no more than ten items on it, and they would be things the kids have learned from earlier grades, such as how to go through the lunch line - although I *have* practiced this with fifth-grade classes when needed!

Your first week of school has lots of expectation-setting sessions; your first month has lots of reminder sessions; the entire year has mini-sessions for new situations. You cannot expect kids to behave in the proper way if you have not explained and shown what the proper way looks like, and held every student accountable for doing it right.

And, if you really want to experience an intensive expectation-setting day, tag along on one of my field trips!

~

If you are working through your student-teacher practicum, you'll still have plenty of opportunities; your expectation-setting sessions will come before you do your first read-aloud, your first lesson, your first transition between subjects, or your first line-up.

Reminders

"Are you meeting expectations?"

"What are the expectations for this activity?"

The question approach is much better than saying, "You are not meeting expectations," because it requires self-reflection. Any time you require a student to reflect or question themselves before responding, you are reinforcing learning to the greatest extent possible - and this applies to curricula *and* behavior.

A Christmas Miracle

As far as I'm concerned, there is never a time when your children are in the school building when you do not influence control over their behavior by setting expectations. I'll cover this in greater depth later when I talk about behavior in specialists' room (such as art, music, or fitness), but it's important enough to make this point now.

You are the primary mentor for the children in your class when they are at school. Period. You are the leader of their little pack, and if you take a break from that role, you undermine your overall authority as the ultimate rule-setter. This means there is never a time when you abandon the behavior of your classroom to another adult. Here's my Christmas story, which makes this point, but also demonstrates the extensive lengths to which you can go to set expectations in order to achieve appropriate behavior.

Every year one of our local philanthropic organizations donates a book to each child in a low-income school. They provide the money, teachers buy the books, and then a few members of this organization show up before winter break to hand out the books to the children. These community leaders loved to hand out the books in my room year after year. They often saved it for last so they could finish up this wonderful charity activity with a good feeling. Why? Well, picture the scene they encountered in most rooms (and which I observed on more than one occasion):

Volunteers arrive to present books. Teacher briefly introduces them and points to the box of unwrapped books sitting off to the side of the room. Teacher retires to the back of the room to check email, ceding all authority and control over her classroom to untrained, uncertain adults who are not used to facing twenty to thirty children at a time. Wild talking, grabbing, and general misbehavior ensue for ten minutes as the books are dispensed, whereupon the volunteers get out of the room as quickly as possible.

Contrast that with what occurred in my room. The set-up was almost as important as the expectations: I wrapped each book (which I had chosen based on the child's interests), put them in a decorated box, and hid the box outside of my room so the volunteers could walk in with it as if they were Santa. But my kids were expecting them because I don't like to leave anything to chance!

What the volunteers experienced was the result of an extensive expectation-setting and practice session. As they stood by my fake cardboard fireplace, warmed by the radiator it covered, the children gathered in a circle on the floor around them with their hands nicely folded. After I introduced the volunteers (praising their generosity), they would individually select books and call out a child's name. Each student would come forward, shake each of their hands, thank them profusely, and walk back to their place without any other noise in the classroom.

After all the books were handed out, the kids would nicely open them and pull out a book that was sure to please them (I had made certain of that). During the excited babble that followed, every one of them took the opportunity to go up, shake the volunteers' hands again, and tell them how much they loved their book with a specific example of why:

> "Thank you so much! I love books about frogs because they are my favorite thing in the world!"

The volunteers then walked out of my room, smiling as if they had just been given a present themselves. And my kids got an extremely valuable lesson in how to be polite to visitors and how to graciously accept a gift.

Have I made my point yet? Probably, but I need to have one more discussion about expectations to be certain.

Getting Students' Attention

I've explained that you can set expectations around any activity that you desire your students to perform. But I think it's important to reinforce that fact with a discussion of a very common question that I get on my website:

"How do I get kids to stop what they are doing, quiet down, and listen to me?"

Well, you know my answer already, don't you? You set expectations. However, you will hear plenty of advice telling you that there are certain magical phrases or techniques that will automatically get kids to listen and that these tips are the only way to accomplish this. These may include:

- Counting down

- Call and response, such as the teacher saying, "One, two, three, eyes on me," and the children responding with, "One, two, eyes on you."

- Clapping

And the list goes on. Which one works best? It doesn't matter! The magic is not in the technique; it's in the expectations that have been set. You can choose any method you want, as long as you set expectations for what the children are supposed to do when they hear it. In fact, you could set the expectation that when you say, "Be as noisy as possible," they will put their things away, quiet down, and look at you. I don't recommend that, because you're kind of working against yourself, but with enough practice, you could make it work.

The key here, as with all expectations, is to go through every single step of what it looks like. Model setting down your pencil. Model turning in your chair to face the front of the classroom. Model keeping your eyes on the teacher, no matter where she is in the room. Model quietly tapping another student to indicate that the teacher wants attention. Then practice. You get the idea.

What do I personally use to get children's attention? I say, "May I have your attention, please?" in a normal voice. I've had more than one principal stare in shock when I can get complete silence in three seconds by simply asking for it.

Again, you decide how the children will act in every situation and set expectations. It's not always easy, but it's that simple.

All About Consequences

Now we get into consequences for not meeting expectations. Remember our overall approach: Build a classroom team to which kids want to belong and from which they do not want to be separated, then set behavior expectations. Most teachers do pretty well with explaining their expectations. The follow-up step, holding children accountable, is where they let their classroom management and discipline plan start to unravel.

But first, a word about reminders.

Reminders

It's not necessary to zap kids with consequences the moment they misbehave, unless you have set a very clear expectation that a specific misbehavior will result in a specific consequence. For example, the expectations about properly managing buckets of water that I set for the buoyancy science lesson I referenced earlier:

> "If you don't follow the steps and play with the water, you will sit out for five minutes during the experiment."

However, most of our misbehavior situations are not that cut-and-dried. Therefore, it is usually appropriate to help students exert their own self-control as a first step by issuing reminders... as long as you don't overdo it.

Pre-reminders

It is quite common to issue a reminder to your group immediately before they undertake an activity they haven't been practicing for very long:

> "What are my expectations for transitioning from math to spelling?"

This sort of pre-reminder is usually quite effective in eliminating problems. You'll need to issue these reminders less and less as classroom routines become more ingrained. Of course, sometimes you will have to go to a whole-group post-reminder, where you back all the way up to the beginning and start over, as I covered in the expectations chapter.

Non-verbal Reminders

It's most common that individual children will start to slide down the slippery slope of misbehavior on their own, while the rest of the class is generally doing okay with an activity. Your reminders to follow expectations may take different forms, depending upon the situation and upon the child:

- A look. Never underestimate the power of a teacher's look! You might want to practice your "look" in a mirror - you'll be using it a lot. My students called my look "The Eye."

- Silence. Going from talking to dead silence in the middle of a sentence will get immediate attention from your class. Every kid who's paying attention will then follow your "look" to the offender, whereupon those group norms will take over, and they will help you get the wayward sheep back into the flock. (Maybe I shouldn't be mixing sheep into the wolf pack! But you understand what I mean.)

- A touch. Tapping a student's desk as you walk by without even breaking your flow of speaking can help redirect in a subtle way that doesn't distract the rest of the class.

- Removal. In the same casual way, you can wander by a student and remove a classroom tool that has become a toy, such as a marker, a personal whiteboard, or even a pencil. Your point will be abundantly clear, so that you can return the item within a minute and the student can continue working.

And, so far, we haven't said a word! The point here is that you don't have to go all black-and-white on consequences; you have a full range of options available to you in the form of reminders that, in actuality, are little tiny consequences for misbehavior.

Of course, if you find yourself constantly issuing the same reminder to the same kids, the incidents will cumulatively add up to the need for a more significant consequence, which I'll cover in a moment.

Spoken Reminders

And then we come to speaking. This is a simple as calling a child by name and asking them if they are meeting your expectations. (Remember, we always use questions to encourage self-reflection.) Next, you ask them what your expectations are. The act of having the child restate your expectations will help them control their own behavior.

Step-asides Save Your Sanity

The key is to establish a *consistent response pattern* with regard to poor classroom behavior choices. This means a response pattern that you implement automatically – but kindly – without having to think through an appropriate reaction for every new situation. Your words are tailored for each issue, but they are done within the context of an established protocol.

The advantage of a step-aside for kids is that they become accustomed to this response pattern, and they understand where it can lead once it starts. If it is administered fairly, once they understand that the pattern gives them multiple chances to correct their own behavior, they become more compliant in working through the discipline process. In fact, many students will come to rely on this process to reset their own behavioral responses when they know they are getting out of control.

Your response begins with a key phrase that the kids recognize immediately as a disciplinary trigger. I use:

"Tansy, please step aside."

The phrase is a bit vague, as it does not say where Tansy is to go - she knows what to do because I have set expectations for the process. Besides, it doesn't matter where she goes, as long as she knows that she needs to step away from the current activity and other students. Keeping it vague avoids phrases that sounds too much like "Put your nose in the corner," such as:

"Shane, please go to the wall (or chair)."

Such an instruction adds public shame to the process ("Oh, look, Tansy has to sit in *the chair!*"), and that is not necessary - or productive - in the least. Plus, keeping it vague allows Tansy a little bit of free will, some choice in where she will go. Some choice is critical for helping kids save face while still complying with your directions.

Tip: Remember your ideal classroom climate; always use "please" and "thank you" even during behavior management situations.

Model this process starting on day one of school:

Step 1: Misbehaving child is asked to step aside to the proper spot in your room.

Step 2: You leave the child for anywhere from thirty seconds to no more than two minutes. You don't have to rush to deal with the issue; the consequence for the student is being removed from the group or activity, and sometimes the student needs to feel this separation for a slightly longer time period. Also, you may be in the middle of making an important point while teaching. But don't leave the child too long; seconds are like dog-years to students; one second in our time frame feels like a full minute in theirs. Don't overdo it.

Step 3: You have a conversation with the student. Ask:

"Why did I ask you to step aside?"

"What are the expectations for this activity?"

"What's your plan for going back to work?"

Notice that final question; they must verbalize *how* they will behave, not just say, "Yes, I'm ready to behave." Stating their method will help them achieve their goal.

If they are having trouble taking responsibility for their actions or coming up with ways to fix them, give them a little more time.

Step 4: Finally, end with a cheerful:

"All right, let's get back to it."

~

If you are student-teaching, you can apply the step-aside process even you haven't been in a position to model the formal steps; it still works because it is simple. Asking a student to move to one side in a calm manner is so much better than raising your voice and interrupting your lesson. Try it!

Apologizing

The final step may also include an invitation to apologize to someone. There are even times when the student owes *you* an apology for their behavior. You should ask the student to provide one (either to yourself or another child), but you must

104

do it in the right way to avoid setting up a head-to-head defiance situation. Saying:

> "I want an apology"

Or:

> "Please apologize to Jeffrey."

… is likely to be met with refusal to give one. Think of how you react when you are angry about being called out on doing something wrong – the last thing you want to do is apologize to someone because you still have anger hormones surging through your bloodstream.

Give the student a little time to cool off, and remember that they like you (if you've been building your classroom community) and would rather not be on your bad side. For a better approach, try this:

> "Natasha, please go find a quiet spot. I'll accept an apology when you are ready to give one."

Then let her think it through while she is sitting out part of the classroom activity. It may take five minutes (which can be an eternity to a young person), but she'll give you an apology – even if it is a grudging one – just to get back into the group. I always graciously accept the apology, reset expectations, and get the student back to learning as quickly as possible.

Practicing on Inanimate Objects

If I have asked a student to step aside for intentionally dropping their chair or messing with my document camera, I will ask them to pat the inanimate object and apologize to it:

"I'm sorry, Mr. Document Camera, I shouldn't have jiggled your cords."

Funny, but effective. It injects a note of humor into the situation, but also helps them practice for making real apologies to people.

Taking a Break

The next level of escalation for not meeting consequences is often a complete separation from your pack for a longer period of time. This should be a rarity and should be administered for short periods of time (use a timer) when the student needs a complete environmental shift to refocus.

It's very common in many schools that students can be sent to a different classroom when they need to take a break from poor behavior choices that they are having difficulty overcoming. It's a good alternative to sending a student to the office, where they may get lost in the administrative shuffle and miss out on too much classroom instruction.

Tip: It's a good idea to figure out the protocol for this when you are introducing yourself to fellow grade-level teachers - before you need to use it *or* before another teacher's student shows up at your door!

I've used this option on occasion when a student is having real difficulty controlling her emotions. Sending her off to another teacher with some work to accomplish (never expect the other teacher to provide this) for up to fifteen minutes can help defuse an otherwise escalating situation. Kids tend to calm down in the other room because they are surrounded by a different environment and children with whom they are not all that familiar.

Also, keep your Special Education teacher in mind; if one of your challenging students has a behavior IEP, then it can be helpful for the student to go to the Special Education classroom to take a break if needed (and if this has been arranged in advance).

Regardless, when the child gets back to your room, be certain to have that brief, unemotional discussion about why they were separated and how they plan to fix their behavior in the future. Also, if apologies are needed, this the time for them to be presented. Do not make a spectacle of the return.

Behavior Management Systems

You may have learned about various "systems" for managing behavior while you were in college, or seen them in use in other classrooms. These can take different forms:

- Moving clips with student names on them to different colored placards that signify different levels of behavior.

- Electronic systems that are projected, with the teacher assigning behavior +/- points.

- Placing counters of some sort into containers to mark off good or bad behavior episodes.

- Placing sticky notes on desks when poor behavior occurs, with a consequence when they total a certain number.

And on and on. I'm not here to say that these systems are good or bad. In fact, I don't think there is such a thing as a good or bad system if it is used in the proper context.

Are there some kids (or groups of kids) who need a more visible reminder? Yes, sometimes, and one of these behavior-management systems can be an appropriate tool for providing that reminder. Don't discount anything that may help you manage your classroom behavior without trying it out yourself.

However, I must caution you about one thing: public shaming. That means holding a child up for the ridicule or negative attention of the group. Now, you may argue that separating a student from the group is the same as publicly shaming them. Well, it's all in your approach. Asking a student to step aside should never be done in a loud voice so that everybody in the room knows exactly what is happening; you help preserve a student's dignity and self-esteem by stating in a very matter-of-fact, often quiet, voice that they need to move to a different area.

You must also manage the other children's reaction; if they begin to draw negative attention to somebody who is experiencing a behavior consequence, you need to nip that in the bud right away.

That brings me to some of these behavior-management systems. A child whose marker is constantly in the "naughty" zone is being held up for all to see as a bad example. Sure, for many kids, an occasional trip to the naughty zone will be enough to ensure that their clip stays in the nice zone. But for some kids, you may as well just write their name in the naughty zone with a permanent marker because that's where their clip is always going to be.

This sort of labeling will not help their behavior over the long term. They'll eventually start to label themselves.

I personally have never used any system beyond the visual, discrete reminder of placing sticky notes on a student's desk. But that's me. As long as you keep the self-respect and dignity of your students in mind, you should experiment with different systems in order to see what works best for your situation and personal approach to teaching.

Just don't make the mistake of thinking that all you need is a "system." As I discussed with the various techniques for getting your student's attention, the magic is in the expectations, not the technique.

The Dangers of Bribery

What REALLY Motivates Students?

Here's the bottom line: In spite of my wolf pack analogy, children are not dogs, and they should not be conditioned to perform for tangible treats, whether food or pencil erasers or certificates. It doesn't work in the long-term, or even in the short-term, in most cases.

Oh, I know how tempting it is! Handing out candy for good behavior seems like an easy shortcut to classroom management Nirvana. Trust me: you don't want to go there. I am certainly not saying that children should not be rewarded – on the contrary, they should be constantly rewarded. It is the nature of the reward that is the key.

Stop a moment and think about which approach will bring out your own best effort at your job:

> A. An M&M, with a promise of an entire Snickers if you earn enough small candies.

B. An unsolicited, out-of-the blue compliment from your boss, who then highlights your contribution at the next staff meeting.

There's no comparison as to what is the better motivator for an adult, and you are fooling yourself if you think that a kid would really, deep-down inside, rather have the chocolate. Try highlighting a student's exemplary work in front of the class and watch that child's face glow with pride.

Do you get the same reaction from candy? No way.

The need for appreciation and recognition is a universal human constant that kids feel deep down in their bones, even if they don't realize it. They want it from their peers, but they really want it from their favorite teacher.

Don't Reward Good Behavior With Bad Food Choices

Another misconception is that a teacher can bring out the best in her students by promising a classroom reward in the future for behavior over a period of time. You know... the, "You'll get a pizza party if you can go a whole month turning in your homework" gambit. Two important points to consider:

First, I said earlier that children aren't dogs... but maybe they do have something in common with them: They respond best to immediate praise, not a promise of a reward in the future.

Second, candy and junk food or drinks are not healthy! Regardless of our own weaknesses for chocolate, sodas, fancy coffee drinks, etc., we all know this is true. As mentors, we have to encourage all that is healthy for kids and that which will help them succeed in life. They may get behavior-related food rewards at home, but there is no reason for teachers to reinforce a connection that is contributing to children's and adults' struggles with overweight and obesity.

Working With Your School

If your school has a building-wide or classroom awards program, then you must honor it and participate in it. It may be monthly "good citizen" awards, or "most improved" rewards or whatever, but if such a thing exists then you need to administer it fairly and place appropriate importance on the process.

But don't assume that this program is all that you need to keep kids motivated and encourage their best efforts and behavior.

In general, institutional awards motivate a small percentage of the kids in a school – usually the kids who would be pretty good anyway – and the tangible aspects of the awards are too far in the future to provide sufficient day-to-day incentive to behave or perform.

~

Full disclosure time. I don't believe in giving kids treats as classroom rewards, but that doesn't mean I don't occasionally give them treats because… well, just because I feel like it.

I don't like a classroom filled with junk food, but that hasn't stopped me from bringing in the occasional sheet cake or bag of popcorn. I never tie it to performance, and I always make sure it is a surprise. I never set up a barter system for effort.

Unique Cases

So: Classroom team in place; expectations all set; consequences modeled and implemented. End of behavior problems, right?

Uh... hardly.

I have devoted tens of thousands of words to classroom management - web pages, blog posts, videos, social media posts, and answers to questions from followers. And I still keep hearing about unique situations that I haven't addressed before.

I really do believe that the pointers I've explained so far will allow you to get on top of 90% of your behavior issues. For the other 10%, I highly recommend checking the written and video resources I have gathered for you on the free resources page: www.ClassroomCaboodle.com/NewTeacher

You'll learn quickly how to best handle behavior in many different circumstances. In the meantime, don't be hard on yourself if you have some rough spots or make a few mistakes. As I outline later in this book, teachers get as many "do-overs" as they need to get it right!

Caring for Vulnerable Children

Something you need to know about working in elementary education: There will be a fair amount of *parenting* mixed in with your *teaching*. It's unavoidable. These small children are with you for six hours a day. It's unavoidable that during those 30 hours a week, sometimes they will need a little mom-time or dad-time for:

- Cuts and scrapes
- Bruised egos
- Social drama/trauma

And their need for parenting may be even more fundamental; you'll need to look out for:

- Hunger
- Hygiene
- Abuse
- Inadequate clothing

- Untreated illness
- Poor vision

... and a host of other items, depending upon the composition of your school's students.

If you don't accept your role as a teacher/parent, neither you nor your kids will achieve all that you hope for. What if you have never been a parent, or a parent of the age of kids you are teaching? You're in luck: you get to practice!

You will find that the need for your parenting skills will increase as the neighborhoods in which you teach get closer to the poverty line. Poverty is a huge factor in the achievement gap between advantaged and disadvantaged students, so let's look at the role you will play with these kids in greater depth.

The Path from Poverty to Success

... leads through school. Student-centered teaching is a mindset that places each and every child in the center of a teacher's attention - a mindset that does not allow any excuse to stand in the way of student success.

There is no lack of data regarding the societal challenges of educating the segment of our population that lives in poverty. The kids from homes in poverty are at-risk students in dire need of drop-out prevention that begins before kindergarten. And from a large-scale, society-wide perspective, states and districts with a large proportion of their population living in poverty can be expected to have lower overall test scores than areas with higher incomes.

But does poverty provide any excuse for an individual teacher to justify poor performance from any of her students? In a word: no.

Every child can make academic progress every year, regardless of their starting point. That is the best gift that any teacher can give a child from a disadvantaged background.

Educational Opportunity

Here is the big picture: The promise of public education is that anyone, no matter what background they come from, can get a free education that allows them to achieve their life goals and improve themselves. When any school fails to educate a child who is living in poverty, our society as a whole has lost an opportunity to create a happy, productive citizen who can make positive contributions to our culture, economy, and vitality - in short, a citizen who can help solve problems, not contribute to them.

The big picture is important, but our focus rests on individual children. Will that kid who showed up this morning from a home in poverty have a better life in ten years? Or will she be well on her way to repeating the choices of her parents and grandparents? Teaching in a student-centered classroom means that *you* make this choice about *her* future every day.

I strongly believe that kindergarten through sixth grade is the key. If we pass a kid on to middle school who is not reading, writing, or calculating at grade level, then he is officially an at-risk student who is very likely to fail, even with extensive efforts at drop-out prevention in high school. Would you want to go to school every day if you were utterly lost because all the subject matter was over your head?

In contrast, if your teaching has played its part in growing a student's skills so that they keep pace with his grade level, then he is set up to really take off in the upper grades. At the very least, he is not working against a stacked deck during his vulnerable teen years.

Making It Work in Your Classroom

We have resources available to help at-risk students. Paying attention to the needs of individual children helps them forget (at least while in school) that they have extremely challenging lives at home. Counselors, principals, and school nurses can help arrange for:

- Shoes and coats. Learning is easier when a child is warm.

- Doctors and dentists. Have you ever tried to focus with a toothache?

- Glasses. Seeing the board is a fundamental requirement for learning.

- Speech or hearing therapy. Speaking and listening clearly is fundamental, too.

- Groceries. So they aren't starving on Monday morning from lack of weekend food.

- Counseling. For emotional issues that may stem from problems in the family.

- IEP's. For targeted assistance, because no one may be working with them at home.

- Homeless student transportation. So they can stay in the same school for continuity.

And the most important part of this student-centered teaching equation, as we've discussed, is your attention.

Where do we end up after all of this time and attention focused on creating a student-centered classroom? Do we still have kids that can be categorized as "in" or "out" of poverty? Not if we are doing our jobs. Instead, because of our devoted approach, we simply have a classroom full of children. Children who are:

- Present
- Warm
- Clothed
- Fed
- Accepted

Now all we have to do is teach like the future depends on it. And that brings us to the next part: high-impact teaching.

Betsy Weigle

PART 3

Classroom Set-up and Organization

She who controls the classroom environment controls the classroom behavior.

~ *Betsy Weigle*

Effectively Organizing Your Classroom

We are talking about classroom organization *after* discussing community- and relationship-building because you must understand group dynamics before arranging your room. The physical arrangement of your room has consequences for how your students learn, interact, and behave. Every classroom is a little bit different. This is because of physical space (for example, how many doors you have coming into your classroom), but also because of grade-level or specialization; a Special Education teacher may have different needs than one who focuses only on math.

An effective elementary classroom layout is the key to keeping your community on track - even if the layout changes weekly. Groups, pods, clusters, rows... I've tried them all. And you know what? There is no "right" answer to classroom layout. Any and all combinations should be employed by the teacher who is keeping on top of classroom management.

You see, individualization doesn't apply only to curriculum and instruction. It applies to the needs of the child, no matter what those need are. Just as some children need a particular approach to learning, some students need a particular approach to seating. And, just as the child will grow and change in his academic needs as the year progresses, his seating arrangement needs will change, as well. Be flexible and always err on the side of what works rather than what you or another teacher believes is an ideal classroom set-up.

The key point is that effective teachers prioritize delivery of instruction and arrange the rest of the room around that. Thus, you won't get a carved-in-stone prescription from me: "Thou shalt do things MY way!" Rather, I'll provide some thoughtful insights to help you plan out the best space for your students and your style of teaching.

The Overall Plan

When it comes to space planning, there are a few major areas of concern in your classroom:

Teaching and Learning. This is, of course, the number one consideration.

The Physical Flow... or how to "get around." This becomes very important when you have a couple dozen children in one room who are all trying to take off coats, empty backpacks, hand in papers, move to and from the front of the room, etc. Without forethought, you can lose precious minutes during transitions.

Accessibility of Supplies and Other Learning Materials. You don't want a long line at the pencil sharpener when kids are supposed to be quietly completing worksheets.

Curriculum Considerations. There are times when your classroom must be arranged in a way that facilitates work groups - conducting science experiments, for example.

Personal Space, otherwise known at as "nooks and crannies." These are areas that allow children to obtain a small amount of separation during silent reading or small-group work. These "extra" spaces also serve another important function: They provide spots where a kid can go to reset his approach to learning. Sometimes a small location change is all that is needed for a student to start getting something done.

Behavior Space. Sometimes a student will need to have her desk a little more separated from the others in order to manage her own behavior.

Your overall floor plan will have to balance all of these needs. Depending upon the space you have available, it's usually difficult to address all of them completely at the same time, so you will be constantly prioritizing. The best guidelines for creating your ideal classroom set-up are:

- Be thoughtful.
- Be flexible and open to change.
- Be child-centered.

It's all about effective learning. You have to put on your elementary-student glasses and consider anything you do from their perspective.

Note: Many of these needs are met by rearranging desks. I'm going to talk a whole lot about student desks in the next chapter, but you can't avoid mentioning them when discussing the big picture. After all, the placement of twenty to thirty pieces of furniture is going to have quite an impact on any room!

By the way, copying other teachers is totally okay. There will be other rooms in the building that have the same physical layout as yours; figure out what's working or not working for your peers.

Tip: If you are student-teaching, then check out as many room layouts as you can and sketch diagrams with notes.

Focusing on Learning

Remember that the first need we are meeting with classroom organization is "teaching and learning." No matter what arrangement you create, you must maintain a gathering spot for all the kids to come forward when you need to teach or read with no distractions. This is an area where all attention is on you, and it's critical for effective learning and creating a sense of community. The focal point of an effective classroom is based upon the community learning together. And *together* means *gathered*.

I only "teach" (as in "deliver a lesson") when children are gathered in my instructional focus area. That is the only way I've found to be certain that all students are absorbing concepts. In my experience, delivering a lesson is not something that can effectively occur when the children are dispersed throughout the room at their desks. This applies to kindergarten through sixth grade - and possibly beyond!

At some point, growth and social development mean that children reach an age where it's not a good idea to pack them closely together on the floor when you are teaching. This is not true for elementary children, however; they like being squished in together (at least most do), and it is critical to get them close to you so you can observe their reactions while teaching. It's a plus that having them gathered about you also means that they are not able to dig through their desks to find distractions. Desks are where children sit to apply the knowledge they've learned and muddle through reinforcement problems while the teacher circulates to assist.

So, with that understanding, let's consider what an effective classroom focal point looks like.

An Effective Focal Point

When it comes to teaching, there is only one person at the center of focus: you.

The focal point in most classrooms will center on a teacher's primary instructional-delivery method. In my room, that's my interactive whiteboard. In your room, it may be a screen for a document camera or a regular whiteboard. It may vary by grade level, as well. No matter how your room is laid out, however, your main instructional area must contain:

- No extraneous, distracting items

- Specific resources for the curriculum being delivered

- Everything you and the kids need to get the job done, because…

When we are all gathered at the focal point, we mean business!

Focus Requires Comfort and Ease of Learning

An instructional focus area should also be designed with the comfort and attention of the children in mind; they're going to be gathered in that area frequently. First and foremost, kids must be able to see, as well as hear. My default desk arrangement - a horseshoe centered on my interactive whiteboard with a couple of outlying pods of desks - defines the learning space by putting a border around it. It's one of the reasons why I'm a huge fan of the horseshoe - it has worked out so well for me after trying many, many options. But if it can't work in your room, figure out how to define your gathering space with something solid that kids can't squirm underneath, like they can with a wide-open table. Define your space with:

- One or two walls (I have used a corner of the room for gathering)

- Bookshelves (make sure they won't move or tip if leaned upon)

- Cabinets

- Desks (open underneath but with the chairs pushed in; they are better than tables)

Carpet areas are almost a *must* for defining a focal point! I am always on the lookout for rugs with clearance tags. I replace my rugs every other year because they get so much traffic and are difficult to clean.

Tip: Get a grass-green carpet if you want to be able to tell your students to "go sit in the front yard" like I do!

Supercharging Your Focal Point

It's all about the students paying attention, right? Having all of the children on the floor is common and effective, but placing students at *two* heights is even more effective - like in a stadium-style movie theater, everyone can see what's going on. So, if you can swing them: benches. You will see an almost immediate increase in engagement. I have three benches in a horseshoe. One of mine came from my school, and two I bought from Amazon (they fold up).

One of the great benefits to having a bench-lined horseshoe is that I can plunk down right in front of any of the desks in the front row to assist and encourage students. It is so much nicer than wedging between two students or kneeling down (ouch!) next to them.

"But… I can't swing benches!"

I know, and I sympathize. When I first started, benches weren't just lying around the school unused, and I didn't have the money to buy my own. Just keep them in in mind for the future; even one six-foot bench will get some of your kids' heads up a level and improve the experience for all of them.

Even without benches, the horseshoe of desks comes to the rescue, at least a little. Some students can sit at their desks, and others can sit on the carpet. Of course, you will have to set expectations that there will be no hands in desks during teaching! My students rotate from desks to carpet - when you build a trustworthy community, sharing desks is not a problem.

No matter what you end up doing, be sure to give your gathering place the attention it needs; it is critically important that every student can see and hear well for maximum engagement.

Your Teacher Desk

I remember some of my teachers in elementary school actually teaching while seated at their desks in the front of the room. Believe me, this is not something you'll see in any elementary classroom in America anymore!

So, what's the point of having a teacher desk? I know of many teachers, personally and through online comments, who do not even have a desk. In the modern classroom, where teachers are on their feet and moving around all day, all you really need is a flat surface of some sort for correcting papers and a place to lock away your personal items. Many make do with a medium-sized table.

Another advantage of a table rather than a traditional desk is that it can provide a workspace for small groups if needed.

Regardless of whether you use a traditional desk or not, it is best to locate it anywhere except your instructional focal point. That's why my desk, and the desks of many teachers, are at the back or the side of the room. My best recommendation: arrange everything else about your classroom to maximize student learning, then find a place for your desk.

Speaking of "arranging everything else," it's time to talk about the other desks in the room: student desks.

Managing Student Desks

I have a lot to say about student desks! They are *so* important when it comes to managing teaching, learning, and behavior. I've already revealed that I favor a horseshoe as my primary student seating arrangement. But that doesn't mean that I only use a horseshoe, or that it's the only thing that can work for you. There are situations throughout the year, from the first days of school to setting up for testing, that require flexibility.

I have seen all manner of different student seating arrangements in various schools:

- Individual desks that can be moved any time
- Table arrangements that are immobile
- Open seating where students carry their personal supplies with them

Any one of these can work. Many times, teachers don't have a choice about the seating arrangements provided for their children, so it's not practical to advise you to use one or the other. I'm going to give you ideas on how to make anything work in order to achieve the best learning environment for your children.

Let's cover several fundamentals of student seating, so you can apply them to your own situation and make the choice that is best for your students.

All Eyes on the Teacher

At the beginning of the year, I often start my classroom set-up with desk groups or pods because it helps build classroom community. Plus, the kids have to sit somewhere, and I need to see how they relate to each other before making decisions about the best classroom organization.

Regardless of how desks are arranged, I make sure that no student's back is ever to the front of the room. This is especially important during the first part of the year. At the most, I'll have them sit sideways by angling the pods. Why? Because, if they can choose, a student will often prefer to look at another child rather than looking at you.

Sometimes, the physical layout of your room unavoidably forces a classroom set-up with children's backs facing the main teaching area. If that is the case in your room, the answer is setting proper expectations. It's not enough to say, "When I speak, you need to look at me." The children have to actually practice how they will pay attention to you:

- Push out their chair a bit and turn toward the front
- Rotate their whole body to face you
- Eyes on you and quiet hands

This may sound like overkill, but I assure you, it is not. Set and practice this expectation as soon as possible if any of your students don't have direct line-of-sight with your main teaching area by simply raising their heads.

Creating Familiar Patterns

No matter what desk configuration you start with at the beginning of the year, it's okay to move individual students or desks whenever it is needed (even the first day of school if necessary). However, I don't recommend altering your overall layout until all procedures are in place. So, if you start the year with rows, stick with rows... with groups, stick with groups.

It's important to keep this familiar structure in place until all of your daily procedures are well established, from getting seated and started in the morning, through lining up for lunch, to putting up chairs at the end of the day. Making significant changes to your classroom set-up prior to "locking down" your procedures will only generate chaos. A word to the wise: It's a good idea to avoid chaos in the classroom if you can!

But a little change is good, too! After your procedures are in place, moving things around a bit is a good thing. Aside from moving individual students due to behavior issues (separating talkative partners, for instance), I play with the arrangements of the desks to keep things interesting. Kids grow and change, and their socialization patterns, change as well. Combining this with the need to accommodate curriculum (a science unit, for example, may require certain size groupings) leads to a shifting pattern of rows and pods all year long.

Adults like their routines, but they also like a little change. We're complex creatures, aren't we? Kids are no different. Mix up your classroom set-up a bit (with a purpose,) but not too much, and keep student social patterns optimized for learning and their interest levels high.

Testing Configuration

There are times when all desks must be separated in order to ensure privacy. Testing is one of those times. Even if the testing protocol doesn't require desk separation, why tempt the cheating instinct? Don't wait to do this until the final big testing sessions at the end of the year; set desks up in testing mode for unit assessments, too. That way, your students will be used to it - and that removes one more thing for them to stress about during end-of-year testing.

Meeting Student Needs

As personality conflicts or the tendency to talk or bother others becomes apparent, the changes begin. Near the first of the year, it's a good idea to give them a heads-up about a big change to the classroom floor plan:

> "Wow... after teaching and learning for the last week, I see a few changes that need to be made so ALL students can focus and learn well. Be prepared for a desk mix-up tomorrow!"

Children will accept these changes once they get used to them. And, truth be told, they usually know the reason they are being moved, so you don't need to tell them. It very quickly gets to the point where I don't warn them at all - they just look for their nametags and carry on.

Bottom line: If desks need to be moved, don't hesitate. If you are in a classroom where it is difficult to move the desks, move the students. Avoid singling out a student who may be a behavior issue; simply move them without comment, whether it's one student or every student.

And rows do have their place, even in our collaborative school environment. No desk organization scheme is off-limits and anything can be tried. Sometimes rows for a few days can provide a bit of "shock value" for resetting behavior. There are also times when kids need to take a break from groups for a bit; many classrooms don't have enough room to make every single desk an island with space all around it, but arranging students into rows is usually enough.

Rearranging

Rearranging should be intentional, as in done with forethought. At the beginning of every year, I write the first name of every child on a small card. Then, whenever I need to rearrange the room, I play "student solitaire" and move the cards around until I find a combination that will work. It's a lot easier to move cards before you start moving desks! After finding the perfect arrangement (or so I hope), I snap a picture of the arrangement and project it on my screen so I can see it as I move desks.

There are situations where a child must move rather than the desk:

- Combo desks where two students sit together

- A rotation-model school where children move to different classrooms for different subjects

That's when classroom seating charts come into play; student and supplies (and nametag) have to pick up and move.

Remember: the purpose of arranging student desks is to enhance student learning. Never decide on a final design without sitting in nearly every desk, or at least every cluster of desks, to understand what the student is seeing and how well they will be able to pay attention to your teaching.

So, who gets to sit in the front row? Everyone, eventually... but some spend more time in the front row than others. As noted earlier, all seats in my classroom rotate constantly, sometimes daily, if needed. But there are special cases.

Arranging for Special Needs

Who might spend more time up front? Students who need more one-on-one, such as my English language learners or perhaps a child with ADD/ADHD or autism or challenging behavioral impulses. Remember that there will always be children who do not fit into the particular style of seating and organization that you come up with. Plan for these exceptions in advance, and they won't cause you to stress out when you encounter them.

This may be as simple as creating some "room to roam" for a child with ADHD, or considering that students on the autism spectrum might be most comfortable at the end of a row rather than the middle, in order to keep their social inputs at a manageable level. It can also mean that some kids *never* move desks once they become comfortable, as doing so could induce unnecessary stress.

Avoiding Distractions

What is the purpose of a coat closet? Storing coats, of course... and not teaching supplies. I'd like to argue for fulfilling the real purpose of your classroom's coat closet, which is storing your students' personal items, including backpacks.

Tip: If you are covering up coat hooks with teacher stuff, you are not allowing your COAT closet to fulfill its true destiny!

Do you enjoy sitting at a desk that has your winter coat and purse hanging over the back? Make room for your students' outerwear and backpacks somewhere away from their primary learning environment. If you are not fortunate enough to have lockers outside your classroom for your kids' personal possessions, then their belongings must be stored away in your classroom closets - if there's any room in your closets! If there's not any room, you end up with coats and backpacks hanging over chairs.

What are some alternate names for such a scenario?

- Personal distraction station
- Aisle squeezer
- Chair tipper
- Thieves' delight
- Fire Marshall's nightmare

Talk about loss of focus! Pockets full of toys and personal snacks cannot be hung on chairs - unless you want to address multiple behavior issues that that will arise all day long, every single day. If there's no storage space available, these items would be better neatly lined up on bookshelves or even on the floor, rather than hung over chairs. Best, of course, is a closet or locker and a firm rule that no one accesses personal items without your permission.

Desks and Behavior

There is so much to say about student desks and seating! That's a reflection on how important they are to your overall classroom environment. It's not the desks per se - it's the students who are attached to them. Arranging the desks means arranging the students. And that, ladies and gentlemen, can have profound consequences.

It's fundamental. Desk locations and the personal interactions that result underlie many, many classroom behavior issues. Assert your control over this aspect of your classroom, and you'll be much closer to having the classroom community you desire.

Here's another one of my quotes for you: "Desks belong to the teacher; students rent them."

The Classroom Community is Everything

Remember, when you've created a classroom community to which children want to belong, being removed from that community is the best way to reinforce that their behavior must conform to community standards. In short, separation is a powerful behavior modification tool. In nearly all discipline situations, it takes only mere seconds of separation, as I have outlined before. However, we all face chronic discipline situations (such as talking), when the child's perspective must be more permanently adjusted in order to help them control their own behavior.

Sometimes it takes a buffer zone, if a child has difficulty controlling his tendency to talk to his neighbors; sometimes it takes even more separation. That may mean moving a child's desk to a separated position (but still in a prime learning zone) for days or even weeks, if necessary.

Proximity = Control

The key is to remember that any child who is separated should be drawn *closer* to the focal point of the room rather than farther away. They already have difficulty focusing, so the last thing you want to do is to remove them even farther from the center of the action.

Once in a while, I must create an "island" for a child who is really having difficulty staying on task. But this island is always located right next to my main instructional area - the area where I spend most of the day. That way, I can provide extra attention to help get him back on task and back into the classroom community as quickly as possible.

This principle is worth repeating: always draw them closer, never push them away.

Although some students put up a little resistance to being placed at a completely separate desk, it's also quite common that they end up liking it because they get more attention from the teacher. That can be an ideal time for you to deepen your relationship with the student so that when he does rejoin a table group, you have a better basis for assisting him in maintaining his focus and controlling any misbehavior that arises.

A Clean Desk is a Happy Desk

I'm a strong believer in the concept that a messy student desk is a roadblock to learning. It increases transition times between subjects and promotes lost schoolwork and homework. I'm not a hands-off teacher when it comes to student desks; my students must keep them clean and organized. As for what belongs in them, check out the upcoming chapter on supplies.

Never hesitate to *gently* dump out the contents of a desk. This may seem harsh, but sometimes it is the only way to get it sorted out. It is a life skill for students to learn how to keep their belongings organized so that they are efficient learners, and there will always be those who find this to be a great challenge.

I will always get a student's permission before dumping, and they are never left to their own devices to clean it up. Many students with disorganized desks need peer or teacher help in knowing what to keep, what to toss, and what to take home. Just like adults!

By the way, apologize to the "connected" student if you have double desks in your room…but don't let that stop you. Once one desk is dumped for clean-out, other students will likely want to tidy theirs as well. If time allows, I encourage this behavior.

And again, always, always thank students for tidying the desks they are "renting." It shows they care about learning and respect their belongings.

All About Supplies

Ah, the joy of newly-purchased school supplies! Who doesn't remember their own childhood back-to-school shopping and all the creative promise that we imagined would flow from markers, pencils, scissors, and glue? Supplies are truly the tools of the elementary education process. As such - like all tools - they must be respected and handled properly.

I've learned a few things about managing elementary school supplies over the years, but the biggest lesson is this: Most classroom supplies don't belong in student desks.

Community Supplies

Allowing each child to keep a full set of markers, scissors, colored pencils, glue, etc. in their desk is like stocking a little toy chest for students to play with all day long. Toys are much more interesting than teachers! It's trouble... trouble you don't need when you are working to achieve great classroom management. So, let's stop this problem before it gets started.

If you have the chance, insert a note into the school supply list to advise parents to not put their child's name on any supplies they send to school. It's best to set the expectation right up front that supplies become community property. By the way, I also don't ask parents to send very much. Personally, I think schools should be providing free classroom supplies, which are simply the tools for learning. But kids do love their back-to-school shopping, so plenty of elementary school supplies arrive every year, regardless.

Note: You may have no control whatsoever regarding the supply lists issued by your school. If that is the case, then adapt the following ideas as best you can.

How To Corral Supplies

Step one: Get some little buckets from the dollar store. Twelve should do. You'll need two or three for each type of supply. Label them:

- Markers
- Scissors
- Glue
- Colored pencils

Step two: If you can, ask a classroom parent to stay for a few minutes after the first bell and help with the avalanche of supplies. You'll be very busy with other tasks, and this can be a first-day lifesaver.

Then, on the first day of school, all backpacks are emptied of classroom supplies, and all items are sorted into the labeled bins. These are put away on shelves for use when needed. You may decide later that you prefer a different approach, such as combo-buckets that mix some or all of the supplies, but at least you've gotten them out of student desks and organized - that's a good start!

You know what's coming next...

Setting Supply Expectations

Expectation number one: You get to say when supplies can be used. All students have to do is ask politely.

Expectation number two: Nothing stays in the desk after a project. Back into the bins they go - properly sorted - and the bins go back on the shelf. Model this the first time supplies are used.

I always explain the difference between tools and toys. Markers, glue, etc., are tools, and I let the kids know that, if they become toys, I'll take them away because the school rules do not allow toys in the classroom.

One of the first-day-of-school stories I like to share is the Tale of Travis. Travis made a weapon out of a ruler and a pair of scissors, with which he threatened me one day. That's when I learned the danger of allowing students to have distractions in their desks! This story is highly amusing to students, but it makes the right point.

By the way, it was easy enough to disarm Travis by saying, "Hey, that looks cool! Can I take a look at it?" He proudly handed it over, at which point I confiscated it.

Supply Separation Anxiety

Sometimes a student will not be able to part with her special pencil box or other items that she brings on the first day of school. Children can be uncertain that they'll ever actually be able to use those beautiful supplies they spent time picking out. If it becomes obvious that this is causing her distress, I make her a deal. First, I have her share at least one item (usually markers or scissors) and allow her to keep something, such as colored pencils. Then I let her know that we'll try it out, and if the box of classroom supplies distracts her from learning or comes out of her desk at the wrong time – even once – it will go home to stay.

Once students see that they actually do have access to the community supplies, they become much more willing to part with their own markers, especially when they start taking up too much room in their desks.

Tip: It's a good idea to plan some small standards-based activity on the first day of school that allows students to use their new supplies. You'll score major "first-day-of-school-feel-good points" with your kids.

Student Desk Supplies

I allow a minimal number of elementary school supplies inside student desks:

- A ruler
- Two sharpened pencils
- A hand-held pencil sharpener (if they brought one)
- Two folders: "Work in progress" and "Stuff to go home"

- A spiral notebook or composition book
- A speller or other much-used resource
- Up to four books to read

Of course, other items tend to sneak in over time, often creating a mess for untidy learners - and you know that I have a problem with messy desks!

The Problem With Pencils

Pencils are the primary elementary learning tool - and potentially the biggest headache you will face on a day-to-day basis. Believe me: teachers have very strong opinions on this topic! The most commented-on question I have ever posted to my followers is, "How do you handle pencil sharpening?" This tells me that every teacher has struggled with the behavior consequence that come from combining:

- Machinery - electric or hand-cranked
- Sharp, pointy things
- A round opening that fits any pencil-shaped object, whether it is a pencil or not

What student can resist spending lots of valuable class time hanging out at the mother of all distractions?

For the record, I'm completely fine with small, personal, hand-turned pencil sharpeners (the kind that holds shavings). For many students, however, they are little more than a novelty that doesn't really keep up with the rate at which they make their pencils dull. So how do we keep a constant supply of sharp pencils for our hard-working writers?

I know from listening to my followers that this area is filled with controversy and different approaches. Choose wisely, but don't allow kids free rein to do all of their own sharpening, or you will be sorry! Here's how I do it.

Sharpening Options

I have tried a few different methods and have finally settled on sharpening pencils myself. I keep an electric pencil sharpener in my room, and I'm the only person who is allowed to use it. No time is lost to students wandering off many times a day to sharpen pencils, visiting all their friends along the way.

It is the job of the students, I explain, to make their pencils dull by writing. My job is to make sure they're sharp. Dull pencils go into one jar, and freshly-sharpened pencils are available in another jar. If their dulling ever gets ahead of my sharpening, all they have to do is ask nicely, and I'll sharpen a few.

After you get settled into your routine, consider other options, such as having an aide or parent volunteer sharpen, or even testing out some reliable students to sharpen them in batches before or after school. Believe me, a child will be much more motivated to strive for the honor of sharpening pencils than they would ever be by even the largest candy bar!

By the way, mechanical pencils are not a good idea. You'll forever have kids messing with pencil lead, and they disassemble into pieces that can be easily lost or misused.

Personal Clipboards and Whiteboards

One of the most-effective student learning tools available is the lowly clipboard. You will never be sorry if you can get a clipboard for every student in your class. Nothing fancy; I'm talking the basic hardboard, brown clipboard.

Why? Because kids with clipboards can take their work anywhere. This can be handy when you allow them to work in nooks and crannies around your classroom, but it is particularly useful when they are gathered in your main teaching area. Having clipboards available in your teaching area means that they can work through examples on their own while you are teaching your lesson. As you'll see in a later chapter, the basic structure of a mini-lesson includes the "I do, we do, you do" process of demonstration.

Well, how are kids supposed to "you do" if they don't have a hard surface to write on while they are sitting on your classroom carpet? Thus, the clipboard.

Personal whiteboards, the size that can fit across a student's lap, are also great educational tools. In fact, I really couldn't teach without them. They're perfect for working math problems, and after the problem is finished, the kids can hold up their boards so you can see exactly what they did. You can use felt squares, baby socks, or little squares of leftover carpet for an eraser.

If you want to be clever, you can have the personal whiteboards double as clipboards by adding a binder clip to one side.

Neither the clipboards nor the personal whiteboards stay in student desks; in my room, they each have their own storage tub. The children get used to filing by in an orderly manner to pick them up or put them away.

Hygiene Items

You will also need to find a spot for some very critical items:

- Hand sanitizer
- Disinfectant wipes for cleaning desks
- Tissues

These are student supplies, just like markers and scissors, and they are super-critical during cold and flu season (which seems to last all year!). I even work the hand sanitizer into my weekly student jobs. The student assigned as "Squishy" gets to pump out the hand sanitizer before we head off to lunch.

Teacher Supplies

Teacher-only items are not usually the first topic mentioned when it comes to discussions of school supply lists. However, it's worth it to note a few important considerations, especially for teachers who are setting up a classroom for the first time. This is not very exciting, but here's my short list of school supplies for teachers... what works for me and why.

Whose Supplies?

Yours! This means a firm rule of "hands off" no matter where you keep them - in your desk or on a shelf, teacher supplies are for the teacher. Without this rule, you will be forever reaching for something that is not there when you need it.

I tell my students, "No touchy my stuffy!" It's a humorous sentiment that gets my point across early in the year.

Here is my list:

Personal Set of Whiteboard Markers

I can never rely upon the markers in the community bucket being sharp and ready for such things as fancy writing on whiteboards or anchor charts. I keep a full rainbow of colors for my personal use rather than just the blue, black, and green whiteboard markers the students use.

Three-hole Punch

Very handy for turning regular pages into notebook pages.

One-hole Punch

Pretty self-explanatory. Sometimes things need a hole!

Scissors

I like nice, sharp, full-size scissors.

Heavy-duty Stapler

This gets frequent workouts because there are always packets of some sort that must be held together, and a regular stapler is simply not up to the task.

Paper Cutter

It can be so much handier to do your paper-cutting on the spot rather than running to the school workroom. Of course, the expectation must be set that this potential finger-chopper is for the teacher only. Generally, I put it away in a closet until I need to get it out.

Colored Paper

I keep a supply of colored paper for my newsletter. Parents learn that when a particular color spills out of their child's backpack, it's something from me that they should read. I can't rely on the workroom always having this color in stock, so I keep my own supply.

Keeping the right teacher supplies on hand can make your job a little less frustrating... and that means a lot on those days when one more frustration might just bring out a scream!

Tech supply tip: An item I have found to be very useful when working with technology is a headphone splitter. It allows five students to listen to one single source of audio. I paid less than $10 for this great little gadget!

The Final Word on Supplies

Are we done yet? Almost! After all of our hard work on the details, we want to be certain that the sum, as they say, is greater than the parts. Our classroom plan must be coherent and cohesive once it's all done, because student engagement comes first... and last... and always!

It's quite simple to confirm that everything is ready: experience it from the students' point of view. As I've said already, before the first day of school or after a major classroom reorganization, I think it is imperative to sit in every seat in your classroom, or at a minimum try out one seat in every table group or area. While you are sitting, imagine the "flow" from a particular group of desks as children move to and from your classroom supplies.

The next step is to keep an eye on your kids at all times. Your students must be learning every minute of the day, so if students don't know where things belong (i.e. supplies are left out), or accessing supplies turns into a giant kerfuffle, then it's time to make some changes.

Nothing in a classroom is "set it and forget it," not if we want every student to be as successful as they can possibly be. Observe, observe, observe... and make adjustments.

Your Classroom Library

I really hope that every teacher reading this has at least a basic set of classroom books for their children to read when they show up to their first job. Even if you do, I will almost guarantee that it will be inadequate. In any event, you will start to accumulate them over time - often, unfortunately, through your own purchases.

So let's start by talking about obtaining books, then what to do with them once you have them on your bookshelves.

How Many Books Do You Need?

Short answer: as many as you can get! You classroom library will become one of your most-valued teaching resources, and one of the things that students love about your classroom. But let's refine that a bit. The well-stocked classroom library will have:

Reading Levels That Bracket Your Grade Level

It is extremely important to meet students where they're at regarding their reading level, even if you are teaching sixth grade and have a student at a second-grade level. Scaffolding the student up through the grade levels of books will be the key to exiting them from their reading IEP. Don't dispose of any lower-level books that you find in your classroom library, and don't hesitate to seek some out as you build your collection.

Engaging Nonfiction on Topics that are Aligned with Your Curriculum

When you teach about interesting topics in your social studies and science blocks, it's natural for children to want to know more about them. That is your opening for getting kids to read nonfiction on their own.

Engaging Nonfiction on Topics of Interest to Children

Your social studies and science curricula will cover only a handful of interesting topics! But there are an infinite number of topics that are of interest to children. A nice selection of animal books, for example, will be engaging to almost any grade level, whether you are teaching animal lessons or not. You'll soon learn what topics your kids really want to know more about so you can tailor your book search accordingly.

Engaging Fiction that Encourages Reading

Just as children like to focus on certain nonfiction topics, there is always interest in a wide variety of fiction stories. Yes, unicorns, princesses, action heroes, and cars - they all have a place in your classroom library because engaging books encourage students to become self-starters in reading.

So, what should you do if you are a brand-new teacher and the books sitting in your empty classroom can barely constitute a collection, let alone a full library? Don't panic! And don't make a giant list of books to rush out and buy. Your best approach? Start buying any books you can get your hands on and refine as you go.

Building Your Library

Here's the simple truth: it is highly unlikely that anybody in your building administration will help you build an adequate classroom library. You're going to have to put out some effort and, yes, some of your own money in order to get your collection of books up to the level where you feel comfortable that most of the needs of your students are being met. Here are the basic book-hunting strategies.

Check Out the School Library or Book Room

Every school is going to have a library, and you need to be fully aware of their procedures for obtaining books. It might be possible that you can check out certain sets of books for your room for a period of time.

Likewise, many schools will have a book room where you can sign out multiple books to use for the entire year. Be warned, however, that a book room might have been somewhat neglected for a few years, and therefore may not be up to the task of supplying engaging reading material for multiple teachers.

Ask Other Teachers

Teachers are constantly switching grade levels, and, as a result, they sometimes clean out books that are no longer appropriate. Any teacher would be happy to have her old books stay in the school and be used rather than end up in the garbage or a thrift store.

Just mention that your classroom library is a bit skimpy and you're looking for any spare books that are available.

Visit Thrift Stores or Used-book Stores

You can often find a lot of titles at thrift stores or other places that collect gently-used books. Hitting several of these locations in one afternoon can yield quite a haul for your classroom library.

Purchase by the Lot on eBay

This is the ultimate of all jump-starters for your classroom library. If you are pressed for time and willing to spend a bit more money, then search for books on eBay. For example, I bought one lot of 125 award-winning titles for only forty dollars - that's a little over thirty cents per title, and they were in like-new condition. One purchase like this can have a dramatic positive impact on the adequacy of your classroom book collection.

Those are a few ideas for jump-starting your library. You will never be done adding to and curating your collection of books. Depending upon the socioeconomics of your school, it's quite common for donations to come in that provide funds for teachers to go purchase books. Likewise, if you manage Scholastic or other book orders, you can build up credits that will allow you to purchase books for your room.

Within two or three years, you will find that you own a great set of books to support your classroom learning environment. You will even arrive at the point where *you* start sorting books out. Please remember to pass those books on to the next new teacher who is struggling to build her own classroom library.

Storing Books

A classroom library has to be organized in some way so it's not a jumble. I cover different methods of categorizing books in the next section, but that still leaves us with the problem of how to group them on the shelves. Since the cover excites kids to read, storing books with only the spine showing is not a good plan (unless they are chapter books - see below). Enter the lowly dishpan.

The dollar store, Wal-Mart, or Target is your source for cheap medium-sized dishpans. Labels on the front identify what's inside, and kids can then easily flip through the texts. Small containers, such as plastic shoeboxes, may be more manageable for younger students. Options for larger picture books, such as those found in primary grades, include larger plastic boxes or even milk crates.

Some Notes on Tubs

Tubs are great for storing and categorizing books, but from a child's perspective, a tub-full of books often looks like just one or two - meaning that many students are not "deep lookers" when it comes to exploring a tub of reading selections. Remember, these are the same children who can't find their favorite socks two minutes after their mom puts them on their beds.

"Seeking" and "finding" are not always elementary student skills!

To help students discover new books, it's a good idea to rotate the selections within each tub every couple of months. Make it a class project, then sit back and listen to the joyous cries of discovery as kids find books they want to read... books that have been hiding in tubs inches from their fingers for months!

Some teachers have room to set tubs at table groups and then rotate them each week. This is another great way to encourage kids to explore new material.

It is also a good idea to display a few books face-out to emphasize their importance. They can go on top of your bookshelves or on your whiteboard rail. Choose books that you have read aloud (kids love to re-read these) and ones that are associated with your current lessons. It's like a store setting up "hot deals" at the end of the aisles - an attention-getting way to get shoppers (children) to buy (read) more products (books).

As noted, I try to have all picture books facing out or in tubs because their covers are so engaging and give students a good idea of what they will find inside. I have organized chapter books this same way, but they take up more space and are harder to sort through, especially if I have a few copies of the same title. Most often, I sort chapter books by level and then alphabetically by author, as would be found in the library. I have students every year who independently choose to be the library manager because they love alphabetizing and organizing!

Organizing Books

What system works best for grouping books?

- By author?

- By subject?
- By title?
- By genre?

Well, all of them, of course! It depends on the time of year, what you are studying, and what you are teaching the children about the use and love of books.

- Studying how to choose "just right" books? Group them by level.

- Comparing fiction to nonfiction? Group them by genre.

- Studying biographies? Pull those into their own section.

You get the idea. No need to be static with your library arrangement. I rearrange my library like I rearrange my students' desks: whenever I think it is needed to meet classroom learning objectives.

I Write in Books!

Only a little bit, though. It is SO worth the time it takes. It was daunting at first because I had a fairly large classroom library. I took all of my books home one summer to label, sort, clean up, and clean out. This gave me the opportunity to see what my library was lacking. After my existing books were labeled, it was easy to label any new books I purchased for the classroom. Here's how to do it.

First, grab a pencil and a book from your library. I'll grab *Enemy Pie* by Derek Munson.

Next, go to www.scholastic.com, and, under the "teachers" tab, go to Book Wizard. Type in the title of your book and select the correct one. From there, you can choose to have the level reported back as a Grade Level Equivalent (GLE), Guided Reading Equivalent (GRE), Developmental Reading Assessment (DRA), or Lexile measure.

So, inside the cover of *Enemy Pie* at the top left corner, I would write:

DRA: 28
Genre: Fiction, Personal Narrative
Topic: Friendship

How about a chapter book? *The Castle in the Attic* by Elizabeth Winthrop is a favorite. The Book Wizard doesn't have a DRA level available, so I will use the Lexile level and convert to a DRA using a conversion chart found online. Inside its cover I would write:

DRA: 40
Genre: Fiction, Fantasy
Topic: Friendship, Middle Ages, Magic

Keep in mind that Scholastic's Book Wizard is not the perfect system. You should read and know every book in your classroom library. If you are uncertain about the level, genre, or topic, read the book and judge for yourself! Who doesn't love reading kids' books, anyway? Sometimes the inside of the front cover will be a busy pattern or dark color that won't work for labeling; I just pop in a blank mailing label (or even a half of one) and label away.

And the bonus? When it's time to rearrange your library, you can have the kids do it! Explain the new piles you need and set them loose to check inside the covers and put them where they belong. They love it, because in the process they are certain to find some books they had been overlooking. And your super-organized kids (there are always a few) will make sure the piles contain exactly what you want.

All that is left is to update the labels on your book tubs or other containers, and you are set to get reading.

Your Teacher Books

Be certain to set your own books aside in a special section of your shelves – preferably out of reach of your students. I'm talking about those books that you use for your read-alouds (both fiction and nonfiction) or other special instructional situations. Keeping them up next to your teacher textbooks or program guides is a good option.

If you let these books get into your general classroom circulation, they will inevitably disappear into students' desks and be unavailable when you really need them.

Decorating Your Room

When it comes to classroom decorating, there is definitely a wide range of ideas regarding how much is enough in elementary schools... and how much is too much. I feel that classroom decorations should be clean and not too fussy. They shouldn't take over a room just for the sake of decoration, and they should be cute and nicely-coordinated, but not overdone. This approach will welcome the children in a positive manner.

Let's discuss a few details.

The Real Purpose of Your Classroom

The lower the grade level, the more ornate the decorations tend to be. There are good reasons for this, including nurturing the needs of little learners. But an effective teacher should never forget that younger kids are more prone to distraction, and this fact mitigates against overdoing the "stuff" adorning walls and tabletops. From kindergarten through twelfth grade, the number one point of anything we do in our classrooms - including decorations - is to enhance learning. Decorations should never be a distraction.

Here's my general rule: If the decorations are the first thing you notice when you walk into a classroom, then I personally think something is amiss. I believe the first thing a classroom visitor should notice is what the children are learning.

A Word About "Cute"

I do like a welcoming learning environment, but I'm not, at heart, drawn to "cute for the sake of cute." It's not my style. Here's the thing: Any style can work. Some will disagree, but I don't think that kids learn better in a cute environment than they do in a merely attractive, well-put-together one.

What makes kids successful? You. As long as the room isn't totally working against student learning, the teacher can make any classroom environment effective. Long after the first impression of the classroom decorations wears off, your students' faces will still light up when they see their favorite teacher in the morning.

Now, I've got to say it: Too cute and cluttered is as bad (if not worse) than too barren. You have to find a balance that suits your style, while staying in the "effective learning zone."

So, there is certainly no harm in sprucing up your classroom look, even down to the smallest details, while you are putting everything in its proper place. We spend a lot of time in our classrooms, and we need to feel at home. But put on your "student viewpoint" glasses before you go cray-zee with cute, and be certain that all of your kids - including your ADD and

ADHD learners - will find a maximized learning environment when you are done.

Classroom Themes

To theme or not to theme... that is the question

I have heard many new teachers ask whether they need a classroom theme. They see other teachers in their building with owl themes, or popcorn themes, or whatever, and they wonder if their kids are going to miss out if they don't come up with something cute and coordinated.

Let's take a quiz. Consider three classrooms:

- The first one has a picnic theme throughout. Checked-cloth bulletin board backgrounds, folded napkin centerpieces at table groups, lines of little ants crawling around the borders of book tub labels, and on and on. It looks like a professional photographer might be staging a photo shoot for a glossy spread in some sort of classroom couture magazine before the kids arrive.

- The second classroom is neat and tidy. Supplies are labeled, but not in a particular theme. There's room to move around, places to store things that need to be stored, well-organized centers, and it overall looks like... well, like an elementary school classroom.

- The third room is in the middle of a third-world country: unpainted cinder block walls, dirt floor, nothing hanging on the walls. No desks, just benches. No paper even, only small pieces of chalkboard for each student. That's it.

Question: In which room will children learn best?

Answer: It all depends on the teacher. Period.

You make the classroom what it is in every way that is important. If you are an effective and engaging classroom leader, you can teach effectively anywhere. If you are not engaging and effective, all the fancy material and centerpieces in the world will not disguise that reality.

So, new teachers, don't sweat the theme if you don't want to. Doing a theme won't hurt anything, unless you are spending time (and money!) that should be spent on lesson planning and the things that really matter. And don't feel pressured to "keep up with the neighbors" in your building. In the end, it's your students' success that will distinguish you.

As you might have guessed, I'm in the second category. Like the majority of teachers, I do like a mini-theme once in a while, especially when starting a new unit. That might equate to redoing a bulletin board, or decorating my door during testing season, or adding some holiday flair. That's fun without being "too much."

Decorating Basics

But, with all of that said, good decorations can be a real community builder because children want to feel good about how their classroom looks. There are certain minimum standards, in my opinion, when implementing classroom decorating ideas. Any classroom should have these items:

- Nameplates
- Calendar
- Room job labels

- Book tub labels
- Supply labels
- Locker labels (if present)
- Alphabet

I say these are a minimum because it's too easy to do at least this much. And it should go without saying that classroom themes that include these items should be coordinated to create the best possible environment. Any new teacher who has put up the items above will really have done all that is necessary to get ready for the first day of school.

Taking it up a notch, the next step is to make your various wall displays coordinate. This includes bulletin boards, the list of your classroom rules, and even your room jobs. It makes me crazy to walk into a classroom and see four bulletin boards with four different (mismatched) patterns. In my opinion, that's like yelling at kids; clashing colors don't do our students with attention deficit disorders any favors.

The next level of coordination is to color-code containers such as book tubs. As with the items listed above, this is not difficult or overly expensive; it only takes some forethought and a trip to the dollar store to buy matching sets.

Keep It Simple

Those are the basic classroom decorating ideas in a nutshell. The fun, of course, is in the details, but I want to reassure new teachers - or any teachers entering a new (and barren) classroom - that following these basics really are sufficient for getting started. Best to use the majority of your energy and time getting your lesson plans ready!

Special Needs and Distractions

When it comes to my students with special needs, I don't even say "accommodate" them - I say LOVE them, and show your love in the way you teach them and attend to their unique needs. We can help out all kids who sometimes have difficulty learning in our classrooms by the way we decorate. Let's dig in a little deeper.

Distractions Derail Learning

Have you ever been in the same room with a mosquito that won't leave you alone? It's not like the mosquito actually keeps you from accomplishing something, but it acts as a constant irritant that makes you less effective at anything you're trying to accomplish (like sleep!). We want to be sure that the walls in our rooms don't create a "mosquito syndrome" for our learners.

Consider this analogy a bit more deeply. On the scale of irritation, who is more affected by a mosquito constantly buzzing around their head? A person with really sharp hearing, or a deaf person? The same stimulus will affect different people differently. My husband is not deaf (at least not most of the time!), but his hearing is definitely closer to the "deaf" end of the spectrum than mine. Consequently, he can sleep through all kinds of noises that wake me up instantly.

Now replace "mosquito" with "clutter" and consider who is more affected:

- A laidback child without a diagnosis
- A child with some level of ADD/ADHD

The incessant "buzzing" of overly-busy walls and excessive decorations will be a learning distraction to the first child...

but a confusing disruption to the second. Students with a diagnosed learning disability don't have the cognitive filter that helps them choose the items upon which they need to focus. We have to help them with those choices in order to enable their success.

Any time a student has trouble focusing (which is particularly true for those students with a diagnosis), then anything we can do to help sharpen the classroom learning focus will contribute to their success. It's not a magic cure, but it is part of the overall solution to increasing learning and retention - and test scores.

Now let's bring this down to an individual level, because even in a well-designed learning environment, some of our kids can still have difficulty focusing. One year, a small boy in my class with an IEP in reading and a low level of ADD kept confusing how to write nonfiction summaries with how to write fiction summaries. I had the appropriate information very clearly written on nearly identical posters, but here's where I made my mistake: the posters were right next to each other.

Every time he looked up, he lost track of which poster he was supposed to be reading and invariably chose the wrong one. It was this insightful young man who asked if we could move one of the posters to a completely different spot so he would physically have to look somewhere else, which would keep him from forgetting which task he was supposed to be doing. It worked.

Our ADD/ADHD kids are just at the far end of the focusing spectrum, but all kids (in fact, all humans) have difficulty focusing in the face of too much stimuli.

Swat those mosquitoes!

Door Decorations

Want to fancy up your room a bit without cluttering it? Then decorate your door! I think of my classroom as a home, and the outside of my door should be a pleasing invitation, just like the front door of my real house. In the eyes of children, that gives my room a certain amount of "curb appeal" before they even set foot inside.

Doorways carry an emotional appeal for all people; they represent passages in life… moving from one thing to another. Use that concept to enhance your classroom community's learning environment in a fun and unique way. Common themes include:

- Current unit of study
- Books being read
- Parent conferences
- Motivation for testing
- First day of school (you'll need to put *something* up on your door for this)

Not feeling the energy to decorate at all, not even your door? Get your students involved!

One winter, my students wanted to cut out snowflakes for our classroom door decorations. I kept saying, "What standard is that related to?" They persisted because the rest of the building had the tissue paper and glitter out. I gave in and allowed them to earn the right to cut out one snowflake for each difficult multiplication problem they solved. (The problem had to be taped onto the snowflake.) The snowflakes went on the door to minimize classroom distraction… and I squeezed a little learning into a craft project.

Don't forget: ideas for classroom door decorations are just a Pinterest search away!

By the way, glitter is a nonstarter in my room, no matter how much my students may want to indulge in it! If you would like to have every item in your room covered with some sparkle, then go right ahead and allow some glitter in one of your classroom projects. One session will be all it takes to enjoy the "sparkle effect" for the next five years.

Putting It All Together

Would you like to see the steps I've outlined in Part 3 illustrated in full color? You're in luck! I've written a PDF book that you will definitely find helpful: *Organizing for the Common Core Part 1: The Visual Guide to (re)Imagining Your Classroom*. You can find a link to it on the free resources page: www.ClassroomCaboodle.com/NewTeacher.

No matter what standards your state uses, it will provide the guidance you need to get your classroom ship-shape in short order.

PART 4

High-Impact Teaching

Children forget what they hear, remember what they see, and learn from what they do.

~ Betsy Weigle

Planning Lessons

Before we get to elementary lesson planning, let's throw a party! It will be a large one; we'll invite about... oh... 25 or so people (about a classroom full). We're doing all the cooking ourselves (yikes!), but we've got some great cookbooks and few websites we really like, plus some random notes from other friends who have done dinner parties.

~

It's the afternoon of party day, and prepping has been a little crazy: scribbles of notes everywhere; ingredients spread all over; a few semi-finished, we-ran-out-of-time dishes prepared. Good enough... time to make it happen!

Party Time!

It's six PM on party night, and the doorbell is ringing. Time to execute our perfect plan.

6:05 - Forgot about the coats! Where are we supposed to put 25 coats?

6:15 - At least a third of our guests seem totally befuddled by the ice-breaker activity. No time to help them... gotta serve the first course.

6:35 - Wow, six guests finished early, while the rest are still trying to figure out which fork to use. And the early-finishers are starting to make blob sculptures from the mashed potatoes. And we're running around like idiots, trying to keep everyone happy.

6:40 - Whoops! There's the smoke alarm - everyone ran outside as soon as they heard it.

6:50 - Everyone is back inside now, but so off-task that they can't play our fun party games. How can a party that took a week to plan fall apart in less than an hour?

What's that? We're scheduled to do this again tomorrow?

Lesson Planning Reality

In elementary school, teachers throw a six-hour classroom "party" every single day. But where was the class in college in which we learned how to transform elementary school curricula in six different subjects into effective, engaging, day-long classroom experiences?

Who showed us how to balance the needs of children when some race ahead, while others are still struggling with the concept? Or the ones who leave each day for specialists and come back after missing an hour of teaching?

And the paper! Oh my... there are 25 sets of everything (assuming we remembered to make copies), and they're everywhere: In piles on the counter, multiple subjects mixed together, crammed incomplete into desks, poking out of backpacks... it never ends! How are we supposed to get it all into the grade book? Or even look at it and give feedback?

Trust me: You can learn to do this! Not all of these steps will be necessary for small-scale lesson planning during a student-teaching practicum, but when you take over full-time (during your practicum or on your first job), you'll know exactly what you have to do.

Lesson planning takes:

- Thoughtfulness
- Organization
- Logical thinking
- Flexibility

This is all made easier if you have a process to follow, and that's exactly what I have for you - as well as a few insider tips!

Lesson Planning Basics

First, if you are in college and there is an expectation to "show your work" on your lesson-planning process, then certainly follow the guidance from your college. If you find their guidance lacking, then augment as much as you need from my process. Likewise, if you already have a full-time classroom, your administration may require a certain minimum amount of documentation for your lessons - don't skip over that.

The Big Picture

From a high-level perspective, here is the lesson planning and delivery "circle":

- Plan the lesson to take students from where they are to mastery.

- Pre-assess student knowledge. Where are students now?

- Adjust your approach.

- Deliver a high engagement lesson.

- Re-assess student knowledge. Did they achieve mastery?

- Plan your next lesson (or unit).

In an ideal world, assessment would occur before any planning took place. But reality dictates that units will be taught on an established timeline within your district, and therefore must be planned even if we have imperfect knowledge. So we make long-range plans and build pre-assessment into them. Adjusting comes from experience... of which you are about to gather a whole bunch!

What Tools Do You Need?

And, just so you know: effective lesson planning does not come naturally, even to experienced educators. I entered the teaching profession at age 35 as an experienced and organized mom with lots of classroom volunteer time under her belt. I had even worked in an elementary school office for two years before getting my Master's in education. I just *knew* that I could make everything in my classroom happen on a perfect schedule.

Well, I'm happy to report that I *am* able to pull off my daily teaching activities with only minor hiccups... but it took me about eight years to figure out how to do it well! When it comes to creating lesson plans, there is not a single system I haven't tried:

- Calendars
- Spreadsheets
- Online planners
- Notebooks
- Post-it notes
- Scribbles on scraps of paper

The system presented in this section is the one that stuck. It's a combination of approaches, tools, and implementation steps that will give you confidence that everything is ready to go and organized for greatest effectiveness. It also allows flexibility for making on-the-fly changes.

Some states and districts provide nice, tidy packages of curriculum and teaching resources all coordinated with a published teaching schedule. Others... not so much, or not in all content areas. My approach is geared toward the "not so much" situation, but parts of it can be applied to any lesson-planning scenario. You decide what – and how much – you need.

Your System

When your lesson-planning system is completely assembled, it will have these features:

1. A way to modify your plans easily… because things change every day.

2. A way to quickly put your hands on what you need… such as hard copies for the lesson at hand:

- Books to read
- Handouts
- Worksheet copies
- Etc.

3. A built-in emergency plan so a sub can (usually) take over without your students losing a day of instruction.

Whenever possible, it is best to have substitute teacher lesson plans that are close to what is being worked on rather than generic, "keep busy" plans. This keeps your kids moving forward and out of trouble, even in your absence.

Computer vs. Paper: Which One Wins?

I'm a tech person. I love my interactive whiteboard. I like having multiple computers in my classroom. I have helped set up building computer labs. I've made great use of student-response systems (aka "clickers"). I use the computer and Internet extensively while planning my lessons.

But, when it comes to keeping my daily "this is what we are doing next" lesson plans straight and ready to go… paper wins. Yes, my lessons are filled with technology, but I have found that the most effective and efficient method for keeping myself on track is my trusty paper calendar and my pencil (the one with a big eraser on the end).

I've got 25 or more kids watching my every move during the day… I can't be jumping back and forth to my computer to see what we are doing next or to make a quick adjustment to tomorrow's schedule since we didn't get through all of today's assignments. In less time than it would take me to walk to my desk, I can make three strokes with my pencil/eraser and be done.

Someday, there will be an integrated classroom management system with a planning app that I can run on my tablet computer that connects flawlessly to all resources, my interactive whiteboard, my projector, and my document camera. That day is not going to be a reality in the vast majority of our schools for quite some time. In the meantime, this system will transfer easily to the electronic world. If you follow it, you'll have the hard part – how to wrap your mind around content delivery – down. Launching an app will be the easy part.

And, if you want to "computerize" portions of this system (such as typing into your daily planning form), then go right ahead. This system is flexible enough to accommodate you.

Effective teachers use effective methods - even if it means going "old school" once in a while!

Calendars and Schedules

Lesson planning starts with the basic foundation of calendars and schedules. You can't plan even a single day if you don't know the big picture of the year-long testing and holiday calendar, as well as the weekly and daily flow of events in your school. When I start a lesson-planning session, I'm literally surrounded by the items listed below. I work at a desk that wraps around me a bit so I can spread out and keep my piles organized.

To get started effectively, you'll need three planning calendars. I have included samples of all of these on the free resources page: www.ClassroomCaboodle.com/NewTeacher.

A Year-long District Assessment Calendar

A curriculum and assessment calendar should block out when different units will be taught and when unit assessments will be given. It should also indicate testing dates for district and state assessments. Such a "milestone" calendar is critical for ensuring that you keep on track with the progress of instruction and don't fall behind. Most districts provide an overview of when different units should be completed. Ask your principal, teaching partner, coach, or mentor for one.

A Monthly Building Calendar

This includes specific notes on holidays, assemblies, etc. As soon as an event is known, it should be placed on this calendar. This calendar should be fairly complete at least two months into the future and ideally will be at least partially complete all the way to the end of the school year. Most buildings provide a monthly calendar; at a minimum, you need a listing from your building that outlines these items. I highly recommend that this calendar be in standard month-by-month form rather than list form; it's visually much easier to comprehend when you are putting together your lesson plans.

If you must make your own calendar, a few different approaches will work. I've kept my monthly calendar in Gmail at times, but any calendar program (such as Outlook) would work, as would a paper, month-on-each-page calendar.

A Personalized Weekly Schedule

This calendar or schedule shows your recurring events. I use a template for this in Excel, but paper would work just as well. It lists:

- Bell schedule
- Lunch
- Recess
- Preps/Specialists
- Etc.

Remember to see my examples on the free resources page. With these basic calendars and schedules in hand, you are ready to start your planning.

Backward Planning

Now that we have the entire calendar framework within which our instruction will fit, we can undertake some backward planning. It is all too common for new teachers to just look ahead to the next lesson or the next unit that must be taught. The effective teacher, however, understands how that lesson or unit fits into the overall picture of what must be accomplished during the school year. Not looking ahead will cause three major difficulties when it comes to the success of your students:

1. You may not finish all of the necessary instructional units, thereby leaving your children unprepared for the next grade level.

2. Your kids may not be ready with the necessary knowledge by the time year-end testing occurs – which is up to a month

before the end of school occurs. Believe me, this does not help your test scores.

3. You may discover that your curriculum is not well-constructed or organized; this could lead you to teaching foundational concepts in the incorrect order, thus making later units more difficult for your students to grasp.

Backward planning to the rescue! If you master this skill, you will set yourself apart from the vast majority of teachers when it comes to lesson planning. So let's talk it through in greater detail.

Backward Planning: The Year-long Plan

When you first sit down to start working on a particular subject, such as math, here is the thought process:

First: When is the end-of-year test?

One step back: When will I need to begin review for the test in the spring? How much time will I need to review last year's standards in the fall?

Two steps back: How much time do I have to teach this subject in-between the review of last year's content and the review before the end-of-year tests?

Three steps back: How much time do I have to teach each unit to mastery? At this point, you will need to consider the content of the units, as some may be more difficult or contain more standards than other units.

Four steps back: What is the start date for each of my units?

This process does not exist in a vacuum; you must consider the unit assessment dates that your district calendar may provide. However, I do recommend not completely trusting those dates. As hinted at above, I have very frequently seen established unit assessment calendars that have me teaching critical units after year-end standardized testing. This is crazy, of course, but if you realize that this is the case, then you have some decisions to make about how to squeeze in critical information between or within other units.

There's one other thing that you will likely realize when you finish this exercise: there is barely enough time to get it all done and no time at all to waste. The practical reality is that you need to start teaching no later than the second day of school. I've known teachers who take an entire week to get to know their kids; I've always felt that, in a school setting, the way we get to know each other is by learning together!

Backward Planning: The Current Unit

We began by applying our planning microscope to the entire year-long process. Now, let's tighten the focus down to the first unit that we need to teach.

First: When is the unit assessment? What standards must students master in order to do great on that assessment?

One step back: When will I need to begin my review for the unit assessment?

Two steps back: How many days do I have to teach this unit before I begin my unit review?

Three steps back: How many different lessons will be included in this unit, and how many days do I have to teach each one?

At this point, you would want to pencil these critical dates into your monthly planning calendar.

Backward Planning: The Current Lesson

And now for the final focus.

First: How many days do I have to teach this standard to mastery?

One step back: When will I start? The date will be anywhere from "tomorrow" (procrastinate much?) to a few weeks in the future if you are planning several lessons during the same session. Pencil the date in. For what it's worth, I like to have lesson plans ready for two weeks into the future.

~

As we narrow our focus all the way down from the year-long plan to the current lesson, you can see that there are fewer items to take into consideration. The other thing is that there is less flexibility at the full-year level than there is at the current-unit level... there's definitely no changing the date upon which your students will take the year-end tests. That's a "hard" deadline. There can be some give-and-take on how long you spend on individual units - but not much if you want to get them all in.

Finally, when you are down at the unit and lesson level, you have much more flexibility to contract or expand the amount of time you spend on any particular standard, based on how your students respond.

Getting Started

Everything I've outlined so far might seem sort of overwhelming... and we haven't even planned an actual lesson yet! Believe me, I completely understand how a new teacher may not know where to begin, especially if they've been hired late in the summer and don't have the luxury of much time for planning.

"Where do I even start?" is a question I got from Danielle, one of my followers. To summarize the process I've outlined above and put it into a real-world context, here's the answer I gave. It also provides a few hints about where we are going next on our lesson-planning journey.

"Hi Danielle!

"That's a very big question, but one that is important to lots of teachers. Here is how I would handle it.

"Focus on one subject at a time. Get out the year-long plan provided by your district and pencil in when all units are supposed to be completed on your calendar. Then check to make sure it all makes sense! What I mean is, be certain that they are having you finish up all of the units prior to when they must be tested in the spring. If not, adjust.

"Then check to see how holidays and breaks affect the plan and adjust again if needed. Finally, make sure you have time in the fall to assess prior-grade level skills and time in the spring for a review. Once you have all this penciled on your calendar, you should be pretty confident that you have the 'big picture' of how this subject should be taught.

"Up to this point, you haven't planned a single lesson, although you may need to review the unit summaries in order to understand what is being taught and how much time it will take.

"Then, work on planning just a single unit for this subject. Start by figuring out how you are going to review/assess the students in September. Then, force yourself to work through Unit One. Print out every lesson plan and every handout/worksheet/assessment. Paperclip them all together neatly so you have bundles of units.

"As you go, write down any questions you have about the unit on Post-It notes and stick them right on the sheet of paper where your question is. When you're finished, you will have a paper-clipped bundle for each lesson. You can store these in a handy dollar-store tub.

"Whew! It's a lot of work, but now you're ready to move on to the other subjects while you let this one rest. By the time you have done this for every subject, you'll have the first two to four weeks of school planned and will know exactly what you need to do next in order to feel ready.

"It is certainly not easy work, but at least it's an organized approach to hard work! I like to get the 'big picture' in place first and then work on a manageable chunk."

~

Now it's time to talk about creating those individual lessons.

Creating Lessons

There are many different ways to format a lesson plan. Too many, in fact, for me to say that there is a "best" way. Instead, I'm going to give you some guidance about the content of those lesson plans and how to ensure that the needs of all of your students are met. As for the format you choose, here are some things for you to consider:

- What system(s) have you been taught to use in college? Are you comfortable with it?

- What does your building principal require? I mentioned this before; sometimes building administrators want to see lessons laid out in a consistent format for all grade levels.

- What are your teaching partners in the same grade level using?

When you consider all options, you'll find one that you are comfortable starting with. And it's just a start; you can change your lesson plan format at any time as your experience grows.

The approach to teaching a lesson (and thus the content of a lesson) plan is fairly straightforward. In general, it will follow the sequence:

As a Group

Gathered in your classroom focal point:

1. Introduction of the standard/goal

2. Teacher demonstrating application of the standard ("I do")

3. Teacher and students working through an application of the standard together ("we do")

4. Students working through the application of the standard on their own ("you do")

5. Giving instructions for individual work and checking for understanding

Individually

At their desks or in small groups, depending upon the curriculum or lesson:

6. Reinforcement activity (such as worksheets)

7. Supporting individual learners to enable them to successfully complete the reinforcement activity

As a Group

Back at your classroom focal point:

8. Review of lessons learned, student self-assessment of mastery

This sequence assumes that you've already done a pre-assessment before beginning the unit. Such an assessment will let you know where you need to begin with your first lesson of the unit, even if that lesson needs to include some review of prior-year standards.

Now let's talk about some of the details that flesh out this framework. We're going to begin with one of the most difficult decisions faced by every teacher when lesson planning: How do you meet the needs of all students in your classroom when some are woefully behind in their understanding and others are quite advanced?

I'm going to include information from my book *Elementary Einsteins: Four Simple Steps to Challenging Gifted Kids in Your Classroom.* This teaching conundrum about balancing the needs of students is central to challenging gifted kids while not leaving others behind. So let's have a discussion about *rigor.*

The Big Question

I answer all kinds of questions through my website and on social media. You would not believe how often I have heard this question, sent to me by a brand-new teacher within a couple of weeks of taking over her first classroom.

"Betsy,

"I just found out that half of my students are at level or above, about half are below level, and three are below-below level. Any advice you could offer? I'm trying to decide how to reach each of these groups so that growth can occur during my direct instruction to the whole group."

Below is my response. It sets the stage for what we are going to be learning in this chapter about teaching to the ability levels of all of your students using only a single lesson.

"Mary Anne,

"You have clearly identified one of the top issues that all teachers face every single year. It's the classic conundrum: 'Do I teach to the low end so the high kids don't get growth, or do I teach to the high end and leave half my class hopelessly behind?' Many teachers make the decision to teach 'low' and assume (hope) the upper kids can make progress based on their natural ability.

"That has never been my way. If test scores are important in your school, you will never be able to get your classroom composite score higher than about 'average' if you follow this path. You *can* meet the needs of all kids, but it takes a philosophical decision on your part more than a strategy. The decision is one that will affect the children you teach for the rest of your career. You have to decide that this statement is true:

"'All children WANT to learn and be smart, and all children have more learning ability than 90% of adults give them credit for.'

"Believing that even your low kids want to learn and are capable of learning comes first. Showing them through your words and actions that you truly believe it comes next, followed by giving them support to achieve high goals.

"They'll take the final step on their own, thrilled to try really hard to live up to the expectations of an adult (you) who loves them and thinks they can succeed, even if they've spent years feeling dumb.

"So, the thing is... you can only teach one lesson. The key is to introduce a topic at a level that is higher than your low kids can handle without support, but that is rigorous for your grade-level kids. Then support your low kids to reach it, while using a few strategies to keep your highest kids pushing ahead so they take their skills beyond grade level."

There was much more to that response – I gave her all the information she needed in order to implement the system in her classroom – but what I wrote above is the critical decision you're going to have to make in order to reach all of your kids. Here is the key sentence again:

"All children WANT to learn and be smart, and all children have more learning ability than 90% of adults give them credit for."

Now, let's break it down and go through it step-by-step so you can truly understand that this is completely doable in your room and will benefit all students, no matter where they fall on the ability spectrum.

The bottom line is this: No regular classroom teacher has time to plan a separate curriculum for each student. Therefore, the key to providing what they need comes down to "support and extend." You teach *one* lesson at the appropriate level, then support your lower learners to reach grade level, and extend your upper learners to go beyond grade level.

Higher-level Teaching: The Concept

Strategy number one is raising your overall game when it comes to lesson planning and delivery. Every year, my administration has been astonished at what I can get kids to accomplish. My secret? Teaching my entire class at a higher level. Let me explain....

It's unfortunate, but a lot of teachers end up teaching to the lowest common denominator based on their perception of student ability. In other words, they start teaching a standard or instructional unit at a level where the bulk of their students are comfortable learning. This limits how far they can push kids by the end of the unit.

Here is how this looks:

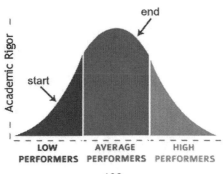

In my experience, this approach is more pronounced in challenging schools. I understand why this happens, since it is seemingly the only way to ensure that lower-level kids aren't left hopelessly behind. For the record, I strongly disagree with this approach.

A more effective approach is to teach to the upper end of the standard and expect everyone to master it, no matter whether they have an IEP or not. Then apply yourself to helping the lower ones get to where they need to be through small groups, one-on-one instruction, and individual attention.

So, while some teachers begin teaching a particular standard at an overly simplistic level and then slowly increase the rigor to full implementation, I tend to start at an intermediate level. I then push the understanding of the standard well beyond what's expected in the curriculum. Like this:

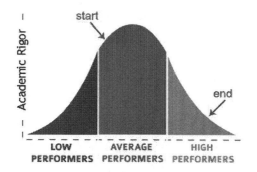

Why is this important when it comes to gifted students? Because if this is your approach to teaching, your advanced kids will *already* be more engaged by your lessons without you needing to give them much extra work to do. Plus, you'll have far fewer issues with gifted kids getting bored and checking out because the work is too easy. But I can still hear one concern, loud and clear:

"How in the world are my lower-level learners, the ones who are on IEP's and below grade level, ever going to keep up with this?"

I have a question for you in return:

"If it doesn't happen in your classroom, exactly when will your lower-level learners catch up to grade level?"

If they are continuously taught below grade level, they will never exit Special Education, and every year they will fall farther and farther back until they are not just behind, but hopelessly behind. You will be amazed at the progress a motivated learner can make, IEP or not, with the right kind of encouragement from a caring teacher and a system that individually supports them.

Besides, crafting lesson plans at a higher level is not actually very difficult. In fact, you'll see that with the approach I outline, no one will be left behind, even though you will *really* be challenging your students' brains - and they'll be eating it up!

It comes down to *questioning, practice,* and *reinforcement.* Let's work through these concepts.

Higher-level Teaching In Practice

So, how do we create lesson plans that raise the rigor level?

This comes down to three basic strategies:

1. Questioning strategies during your mini-lesson

2. High-level practice items to work through as a group

3. Practice/reinforcement activities (such as worksheets) that include problems that require greater mental effort

Questioning

Your goal when teaching your mini-lesson is to stretch your students' brains beyond the actual standard you are teaching them. We do this largely by asking questions. You can adapt the following questions to nearly any lesson:

"Why do we need to know this?"

"Why is this so important that we are going to spend a week learning it?"

And then, as you work through activities during your lesson:

"How do you know this is the right answer?"

You can see that we are expecting children to think more deeply about everything we are teaching. It's not enough for them to be able to execute the standard of the lesson; they need to be able to verbalize the *how* and *why* in order to really sink their teeth into it and be engaged.

Practice

When you work through examples with the class, starting with the basic standard is perfect - for a beginning. Before kids head back to their desks for independent work, however, they need to noodle through a practice question that raises the stakes a bit.

- In math, you add a trifle more complexity.

- In reading, you work through a more difficult piece of text together or ask high-level questions that go beyond the words in the text.

If you are having difficulty figuring out what "a little more complexity" looks like, Google your standard: "Adding single digits examples" or "Finding main idea examples." You'll be able to glance at the results and see right away which examples are easy and which are harder.

Reinforcement

And now for the reinforcement activities. This includes the worksheets your kids head back to their desks to complete, whether they be math problems or a paragraph of text to consider. Often, you will be provided with these reinforcement activities as part of the curriculum. But just because they are provided doesn't mean that they are challenging enough for *your* students!

For this, you will have to rely upon your teacher insights, your knowledge of your students, and some plain old common sense. You can tell when looking at reinforcement activities if they are only covering the exact standard being presented in the lesson. If they are, then you should add a few items that stretch your children's learning further.

Perhaps, in math, that includes a couple of problems that involve multiple digits or combine a previously learned operation with the current standard. For example, expecting the students to do addition (previously mastered), as well as multiplication (currently being taught).

In reading, you may ask students to expand their analysis of "main idea" (for example) from a short paragraph to a two-paragraph selection.

You get the idea: We are taking a basic lesson plan and juicing it up a bit by...

- Asking tougher questions

- Practicing a couple of harder examples

- Doing reinforcement work that includes more than the basics

The next step is individualizing (covered in a moment) to help your lower students strive for and meet these challenges, while your higher-level students are naturally more engaged.

But even when individualizing, the stretching of your students' brains never stops! As you walk around the room, your questions keep pushing the learning:

> "That's awesome, Brian! How do you know you got the right answer?"

And so on. At every step, during every moment of the day, you are pulling your children's thought processes higher and higher. Our ultimate goal is that assessments should be easy-peasy for our students because they've already mastered standards beyond what is going to be tested.

In an ideal world, your kids should complain to you that the tests you give are too easy! (And I have had this happen - even on the state assessment!)

Individualizing Built Into Every Lesson

Now we've got the foundation in place: beginning our instruction at a higher level, which allows us to push our entire class (gifted *and* IEP kids included) farther along before we wrap up our unit. But this solution doesn't work without the individualized support that I've been talking about. And that support comes from using your classroom equivalent of my "circle table."

For years, I had an old poker table at the back of my classroom. It was covered with a hard writing surface and surrounded by stools so that multiple kids could easily fit around it. Of course, any table will work; it's the *concept* of the circle table that's important - although my kids always liked the fact that they were gathered around a poker table!

So, how does this fit in with your mini-lesson?

At the end of every lesson, I announce that those who want a little bit of extra help need to meet me at the circle table with their papers. This is my opportunity to very quickly clear up any lingering issues that a child may be having with understanding the lesson.

By the way, if I get a flood of people at the circle table, then I know that I need to do some immediate re-teaching!

Usually, these kids just need a little confidence. After giving them a quick brain boost, I'm free to walk about the room, asking questions and checking in to see how everyone is doing, including those advanced kids who may be racing ahead already.

Then the circle table comes back into play if needed. If your speed-demons are finishing up, they can be called back for a quick review of their work and then some extension activities.

The real key here is that a mini-lesson should really be a "mini" lesson. Extra talking doesn't mean the kids are engaged in extra learning. Introduce an easily-digestible portion of a standard and get those kids working on it. That gives you the time to support and individualize so that all of the kids in your classroom can be successful.

Left Behind? Or Pulled Ahead?

I can understand if you remain concerned about your lower kids being left behind because of the methods I've outlined. However, I really encourage you to try it; it will resolve not only many of the issues with your early finishers, but will also raise the performance of all the kids in your room. After all, isn't that really the point of Special Education: supporting kids to function at grade level?

Trust me on this: challenging lesson plans with support from a devoted teacher can work wonders!

I have a lot more ideas on this, including information on different subject areas, in my *Elementary Einsteins* book.

So, there you have it: the overall concept of how to structure a lesson plan, no matter what format you choose. I'll finish this chapter with a few more guidelines that take lesson plans from "adequate" to "super-engaging."

Children Learn by Seeing and Doing, Not by Listening

Humans are primarily visual learners. Yes, there is always room – and good reason – to include other learning pathways, such as auditory or kinesthetic. But make no mistake: your children will learn much more quickly if you engage them visually.

We've all heard the voice of the teacher in the Charlie Brown cartoons... you know, the voice that is essentially a nonsensical drone. No matter how great a lesson you prepare, this is exactly how your voice sounds to your students after approximately five minutes.

Let me restate this to ensure full understanding: You cannot *talk* knowledge into students' heads. They must *see* and *experience* to learn. By the way, this is why I absolutely adore using interactive whiteboards - and why my students love them as well.

So keep it visual, keep any talking short, and move on to practical application. As I've said, this is why mini-lessons are "mini" - they're supposed to be short so that kids can quickly start applying what they have learned in order to reinforce it.

The Pre-assessment

I've tossed out the concept of a "pre-assessment" a few times as a means for determining the current level of knowledge your students have regarding a particular standard. Such an assessment, given before your first lesson in a unit, can help you target your instruction so that you are not making assumptions about your students' existing knowledge.

Where do these pre-assessments come from? Many curricula will have these built in, just as they have pre-tests built into the review section for each unit. If they don't, then look up your standard online and find a set of practice items.

Remember: This pre-assessment is for your information; it doesn't have to be long and involved, just long enough to let you know the current mastery level of your students.

Usually, you'll be giving this pre-assessment near the end of the preceding unit. You want to hit the ground running with your first lesson in your next unit, so don't take up that valuable time with your pre-assessment... get it done a few days earlier so you can do some final tweaking on your lesson plans.

Delivering Lessons

You've done your backward planning, examined your calendars, and finished the hard work of creation; you now have a lesson plan that is ready to deliver. This is where the "rubber hits the road"; this is the point where your students increase their knowledge... or not.

If you followed my advice, you've already incorporated engaging activities into your lessons such as technology, video, interactive whiteboards, small-group work, etc. But all of that can fall apart if you, the teacher, feel disorganized in your delivery or become frazzled when things don't go as planned. So, let's address the process of delivery.

I said earlier that a lesson will generally follow this sequence:

As a Group

Gathered in your classroom focal point:

1. Introduction of the standard/goal

2. Teacher demonstrating application of the standard ("I do")

3. Teacher and students working through an application of the standard together ("we do")

4. Students working through the application of the standard on their own ("you do")

5. Giving instructions for individual work and checking for understanding

Individually

At their desks or in small groups, depending upon the curriculum or lesson:

6. Reinforcement activity (such as worksheets)

7. Supporting individual learners to enable them to successfully complete the reinforcement activity

As a Group

Back at your classroom focal point:

8. Review of lessons learned, student self-assessment of mastery

Correcting papers and self-assessing *yourself* comes after, which I will talk about in the next chapter.

Let's go through this process step-by-step and flesh out some details. First, however, a few notes on what to do with the stacks of paper you have created.

Storing Lesson Plans

When you have finished your lesson-planning process, you will undoubtedly have several packets of paper: paper-clipped, binder-clipped, Post-It-noted, and rubber-banded. The last thing you want to be doing when you have a classroom full of children staring at you is rummaging through your lesson-plan piles looking for what to do next. That will get you flustered before you even begin.

What you need is a little bit of organization. What you need is another tub from the dollar store!

As noted before, I've always tried to stay two weeks ahead on completely-prepped lesson plans. I've heard teachers say that they like to plan out through the end of the unit, and that's fine, but as you are approaching the end of the unit you'd better be doing some planning on the next one! Thus, my two-week guideline.

Once these lesson plans are ready, I place them into my "two-week tub." This is a dollar-store dishpan with dividers for days of the week. Everything for the next teaching day goes behind the appropriate divider in the order in which it will be taught. In other words, if my teaching schedule goes "math, reading, spelling, social studies," then the lesson-plan packets for each of those curricular areas are placed in that order behind the appropriate tab for the day. The rest of the two-week plans are stored in a similar way.

You can immediately see the advantages:

- The tub keeps everything in one place, as opposed to spread around the room.

- It can be carried about as needed without jumbling the contents.

And the big one:

- When it's time to teach the next subject, I know exactly where to go and exactly what to grab without any fumbling.

I'll get into this more a bit later, but it also provides huge dividends when a substitute teacher takes over your classroom and needs to carry on with teaching your lesson plans.

The Mini-lesson

The mini-lesson is the big debut of your lesson plan. I've already cautioned you about ensuring that the lesson is "mini" to stay within the attention span of your students. If you are introducing only one concept, then the lesson shouldn't need to be overly long. If it's longer than fifteen minutes, no matter how great the lesson is, you will lose their attention. Now, let's talk about the mechanics of lesson delivery.

In order to ensure that all attention and focus is on you – and to ensure that you have quick behavioral control – students should be gathered in your main teaching focal point before beginning. You'll be working on some problems together, so have them bring personal whiteboards and markers or clipboards and pencils. This is important even if you'll have some kids working in front of the group on the whiteboard (interactive or not) - remember: to retain it, they need to do it.

1. Introduce the Standard/Goal

Start by telling your students what they are going to learn. This includes the learning target (the standard) for the lesson and also an introduction with a real-world example. For example:

> "Today we are learning about inference, which is how to understand what an author - or even one of your friends - might mean even if they don't write it out or say it."

Tell them why you are going to learn it.

> "It's important to understand the meaning behind the words in order to fully understand what someone is communicating to you. Without this understanding, you might miss out on a whole lot of information."

Then have them turn and talk to a partner to restate the goal of the lesson in their own words.

After this introduction, dive into your lesson plan. After a more in-depth introduction of the concept, including examples they can see, you'll proceed to the "I do," "we do," "you do" portion for applying the standard. This means that you demonstrate, then you all work through a problem together, then the students work through one on their own.

2. Demonstrate Application of the Standard ("I do")

Work through an example, using your document camera or the whiteboard so that all can see your process.

3. Work Through an Application of the Standard Together ("we do")

Have the students work an example that is similar to the first one on their personal whiteboards, while talking you through how to do it. Make sure everyone can see you work your example.

Have the students work an example that is harder than the first one (raising the rigor) on their personal whiteboards, while talking you through how to do it, for all to see.

4. Have the Students Work Through the Application of the Standard on Their Own ("you do")

Finally, every student works through an example on their own, using personal whiteboards or clipboards. They can hold up their work when they are done so that you can see if they have mastered the concept. Be ready to do more than one problem this way if you see that understanding is lacking. And don't hesitate to up the stakes a little with a more rigorous problem.

Finally, have your kids share, in their own words, what they have learned.

5. Give Instructions for Individual Work and Check for Understanding

Provide instructions and expectations for how to complete the independent work when you break up the mini-lesson, and have a student repeat those instructions in her own words. Then off to their seats (or small groups) they all go.

Really? All That in 15 Minutes?

You may be thinking that there is no way that this can all be accomplished in 15 minutes. But if you do your mini-lessons the same way in every subject area every day, the children will quickly get into the routine. You will be amazed at the amount of content you can cover - with very high engagement - when everyone learns and follows an efficient learning process. Essentially, you are setting an expectation for how your lessons will go and, with practice, your students will conform to those expectations.

Independent Work

6. Start the Reinforcement Activity (such as worksheets)

The work that students undertake independently after the mini-lesson is designed to cement in their minds the concepts you have taught by way of practical application. Often, this is a worksheet, whether it be math problems to puzzle through or reading selections to parse and analyze.

Remember what I keep saying about rigor! It's this independent reinforcement activity that will scaffold your students from basic understanding up through more advanced and difficult application. A child who works his brain harder – even harder than is required for grade-level standards mastery – will better remember the concept than one who has done the bare minimum.

I know I harp on this a lot, but remember that your kids are smarter than so many adults give them credit for. And, with the support of a dedicated teacher, they can achieve amazing things. These amazing things occur because of you! This is the moment in time where you pull kids to higher levels of learning than many teachers feel is possible.

7. Support Individual Learners to Enable Them to Successfully Complete the Reinforcement Activity

This is where my circle table comes into play. Some kids will need to head back to your one-on-one focus area right away after a lesson, and that's okay. You will often find students who can do the independent work immediately, but they lack confidence. A lack of confidence can be just as debilitating in gaining knowledge as a lack of understanding. Great teachers provide knowledge *and* instill confidence.

I've said this before, but how much would you have loved for all of your teachers to tell you repeatedly how confident they were in your success? If every adult role model in your K-12 academic career had looked you in the eye and said, "I believe in you," wouldn't that have made you feel like the smartest person in the school?

Circle-table work is very brief. You're not there to do the work for the students, of course, so your conversation starts with having them share what they are confused about, then working an example together. Immediately after, they do an item on the worksheet on their own so that you can pinpoint any mistakes they are making and correct them. Then back to their desks they go to continue muddling along on their own.

You are then free to circulate the room, checking in on and helping other students. You should always have a "hot list," either in your head or written down (if you need a reminder); essentially, you need to know who needs your extra support based upon:

- How they were grasping the mini-lesson
- The results of their prior work in the subject
- Their status as an English language learner
- Whether or not they have an IEP in this subject

But don't focus only on those kids; during your drive-by's, make sure you give plenty of pats on the back and encouragement to everyone. And use those questioning strategies rather than handing out answers or meaningless compliments.

Finishing the Lesson

8. Review Lessons Learned, Have Students Self-assess Mastery

After independent work, pull the students back together for a period of self-reflection that will further cement what was learned. Ask:

"What was our goal today?"

Then:

"How are you doing on achieving this goal? How do you know?"

I have my kids give themselves a numerical ranking by holding up their fingers with a three, two, or one:

1 = I still need help
2 = I'm getting there
3 = I've got it

Ask the children:

"How do you know if you have mastered this topic?"

"Do you feel like you're ready to teach this to someone else? How do you know?"

You may find, during this mini verbal assessment, that there is still work that your entire class needs to do to achieve mastery. This will be further clarified when you check their independent work, which we will consider in the next chapter.

Rinse and Repeat

Does that whole process seem sort of intense? Well, that's because it is! Learning new concepts is an intense process, but, really, it boils down to the following steps:

- Introduce a small portion of something new
- Work on it together a little bit
- Work on it alone with support
- Review what's been learned

What I have shown you are the practical steps in carrying out the "gradual release" method of learning. It seems intense because it is very *intentional,* and there are no wasted steps. And believe me, there is no time for wasted steps in an elementary teacher's life!

Kids, like all humans, love routines. This is nothing more than a routine that you establish about how teaching and learning occur in your classroom. Your students will get on board almost immediately, and you will be amazed at how quickly you can move them to higher levels of mastery - and how much content you can cover!

Assessing and Reflecting

As I said before, data analysis is the new norm in teaching. Data can be abused, but can also be incredibly helpful to an individual classroom teacher who is seeking to maximize her impact on student learning.

How does an individual teacher collect data? Well, obviously, from quizzes, tests, and assessments. But there is a lot that can be learned - and quickly implemented - by simply correcting papers. Insights gained from correcting student work will impact your future lesson plans as you modify them to ensure mastery of standards. Data can do more than guide your next few lesson plans, however; it can also help you to deliver better and more engaging lessons year after year *and* improve your overall abilities as a professional educator.

Let's get into those details.

Correcting Papers

We've already undertaken a little bit of data collection by asking students to self-assess their level of mastery at the end of our lesson, so we have some idea of how well they "got it." The proof - one way or the other - will come from the independent work they did. But to get this valuable data, you have to actually look at it.

"Well, no kidding!" you may be thinking. But there are a very large number of teachers who do not review every piece of work that students complete. I have an issue with this, as you might imagine!

I strongly believe in correcting every single item on every single paper that a student completes. I believe that if you mark a paper as "complete" without looking at it, then you are not honoring the work that you ask students to do. You are also giving up a huge opportunity to assess mastery.

How would you feel if your boss (in any job) asked you to spend your valuable time on an assignment, then put a check mark on it and handed it back without reading it or commenting on it? Worse, what if he did this repeatedly, then one day nailed you for making a mistake - a mistake you had been making for weeks and that he could have corrected early on? This is the very definition of demotivation. So, I check every item on every paper.

The Paper-correcting Process

I start by sorting all of the papers from a single assignment so that they are together. Then I put the answers very briefly on a sticky note on the top so that I can correct a few at a moment's notice.

Usually, I'll get the homework corrected after attendance is taken and the children are working on the entry task. During lunch, I will often get the papers from the morning assignments done (I've never been one to hang out in the teachers' lounge during lunch - too much to do!). During preps or breaks, I'll often be able to get the rest done. Diligently using these little slices of time keeps me from taking most papers home to correct...

... except for writing and some reading assignments. It takes too long to correct and provide feedback on them, so home they go - but at least they are not accompanied by papers from math, spelling, and other subjects.

Most corrected papers will go into student mailboxes for them to grab before they go home. However, when it's clear that some students need extra attention on a topic, those papers are bundled up so that I can pull kids aside for a review. This individual attention should happen within 24 hours, if at all possible, so the concept is still fresh in their minds. Once they rework the incorrect items, they can turn them in again for a final review.

The Problem With Packets

Ah, the convenient, efficient homework packet, the solution to every busy teacher's need to "give the kids something to do at home" and placate parents who insist on homework. Just staple together a bunch of worksheets (that may or may not relate directly to the current lessons), send them out on Monday, retrieve them on Friday, and then throw them in the garbage. Oopsie! My anti-packet bias is showing, isn't it?

Okay, to be fair, most packets don't end up in the garbage, but they may as well. Consider that each packet will have at least five pages in it, often more. Consider also that the mathematical probability of a teacher correcting 25 x 5 pages of homework over the weekend has been scientifically proven to be a negative number. Which is why most packets end up with a check mark for "complete" and not much else.

It's harder to do, but if homework is given out at all, it should reinforce what was learned in class the day it was handed out, so that it acts like a final check on whether the lesson "stuck." And if it didn't stick, then that issue needs to be addressed immediately, not a week later.

Providing Student Feedback

Correcting papers does much more than provide data for teachers - it provides performance feedback for students. When you think about it, it's a constant feedback loop: students are working on concepts all day long and getting a steady stream of feedback from their teachers.

This is for more than the students, of course; feedback is very important for parents, as well. One of my son's elementary teachers had a policy of holding all corrected papers until the parent/teacher conference. It was not pleasant to discover that he had been struggling in a particular subject for a while. Note: Don't do this. It's a great idea to keep some papers to show evidence of student growth and mastery at conferences, but not *all* of them. If necessary, make a copy of ones that parents really should see right away but that should also go in a student's conference folder.

Knowing the importance of a corrected paper, you can see that your feedback comments are very important. Here's my general rule: Always provide feedback in the form of questions. We want students to rework the items to arrive at the correct answer on their own so that they internalize it.

216

You're just giving little hints to send them down the correct path.

What Goes into the Grade Book?

Every single score on every single paper? Only the unit assessment? It depends on the district and the school. This is an area to clear up with your principal *before* you have a giant pile of papers to enter in a panic right before report cards are due!

Applying Student Data

Now that we've collected data and even taken some immediate steps to use it (circling back with certain students and sending papers home), we must consider how this data will impact our future lessons. In the ideal scenario, you'll find that there are only a few kids who had difficulties, whom you can work with individually to bring them to mastery. Is quite common, however, to find a trend that many of your students are not "getting it."

In that situation, you will need to decide what to do. Never just move on; you can't leave a building block that will crumble when you place other levels of knowledge upon it. Here are your options:

- A quick review of a particular part of the standard that seems to be the sticking point

- Re-teaching the entire lesson, taking a different approach

- Pulling small groups so you can give kids almost one-on-one attention to bring them up to speed

- Adding some problems to their entry task (bell work) in order to provide reinforcement

Some of these approaches may impact the content of your future lesson plans, while others may simply need to be squeezed into your routine.

It's not always a case of, "Why did they struggle?"; you may find upon reflection (and upon considering their individual work scores) that your kids got it right away. If they are flying through a concept, don't belabor it... move on to the next standard in the unit - but ensure that you have appropriate reviews in the future to be certain that their mastery "stuck."

Likewise, you may find that backing up and re-teaching a prior standard is necessary - even if it's a standard from an earlier grade level. There is no point in trudging forward if the kids aren't learning.

Testing Attitudes

So far, we have discussed your informal assessments of both your kids and yourself. But all of this content delivery is, of course, leading up to regular formal assessments in the form of unit tests or year-end testing.

There's one thing that you need to understand about testing in the modern teaching environment: It may be excessive, but it's also very important. Put simply, your students' success will be gauged on how well they test, and it will eventually affect their ability to graduate from high school. Of course, your own evaluation will rest upon the success of your students on various tests, as well. So, whether you agree or disagree with the amount of testing, I believe that it is important for teachers to support and encourage their children to do their absolute best in testing situations.

Picture an elementary classroom getting ready to take a test. It may be a spelling quiz, a math unit assessment, or a comprehensive year-end test - it doesn't matter. In our first scenario, the teacher explains the following in a monotone, everyday voice:

> "All right, everybody, do your best. Try your hardest and finish on time - we don't want to be late to lunch."

In the second scenario, the teacher's tone is more animated, but in a negative way:

> "We've studied this, so everyone should know it. Don't make those same silly mistakes we've been correcting over and over - you know better."

In our last scenario, the teacher is bubbling with excitement:

> "Show me what you know, people! Every one of you is TOTALLY ready for this. I can't wait to see how smart you are!"

It's pretty obvious which scenario will produce the best results, isn't it? With just a few words, the third teacher has transformed her students into eager participants in the challenge of demonstrating what they have learned. More importantly, she has given them a very motivating reason to try hard: the kids want their favorite teacher to be as proud as they are of their work.

Remember back to the discussions on team-building - you are the leader and mentor and alpha of your pack. Your little cubs want your approval, and they will strive to achieve the things upon which you place importance. A great team-building speech will not replace solid instruction, but it can move the average results up by several points.

Someday your children will (hopefully) grow into self-motivated adults who desire to excel on life's tests for their own intrinsic reward. But, with rare exception, this will not be the case during their elementary years. Therefore, you have to give them a reason to try their very hardest - if no one else cares about the result, why should they?

And caring is infectious; once you show a student that you are excited about their scores, they will begin to generate their own internal excitement, as well.

Summative Assessments

Up to this point, you have been using formative assessments to guide your instruction, some as informal as looking over their shoulders while they work and some a bit more formal, such as grading homework and spending one-on-one time. Of course, at the end of every unit, there will be a summative assessment. Here's how I feel about these:

You should always know exactly how your students will score on a unit assessment before you give it.

The unit test is not something that is sprung on the kids on a set date, whether they are ready or not. We aren't teaching college courses! Rather, it is given to them when you know they are absolutely ready to ace it. You'll know this through your continuous feedback loops, as outlined in this chapter. You'll also give them a practice test a couple of days before the final unit assessment. You'll know right away if you have more work to do to ensure that they have completely mastered the subject before giving them the assessment that goes into the grade book.

Children really appreciate a teacher who works extra hard to ensure that they achieve great scores on tests. When they know that you are completely dedicated to helping them achieve at a high level, it removes a whole lot of testing anxiety. That alone will raise their test scores.

Planning For Future Lessons

Now it's time to undergo your own reflection for self-improvement. Before storing your lesson plan away, consider the following and make notes:

- What questions or misconceptions did the children have about the topic before you even began teaching? Can you introduce the standard in a different way next time to clear their path to understanding?

- What were their stumbling blocks as you went through the lesson? Did they result from an unclear approach you took to teaching? What's another way to teach the same thing?

- If the lesson was too long, why was it too long, and how can it be changed to make it shorter?

Remember, if the children didn't get it, it's pointless to simply repeat the same lesson.

Make notes on the original lesson plan so you have them for the following year. In my case, my lesson plans are all stored on my computer, so I make notes there. If you are sticking with paper, then use as many sticky notes as you need to be sure you don't forget your valuable insights.

Teaching is Hard Work!

Wow... we've reached the end of the lesson planning, delivery, and assessment cycle. It's a ton of work and attention to detail, isn't it? And this process is being implemented for multiple subjects, all day long, every day. But these are all vital steps in learning, and if you leave some out, your students will not make the progress that they deserve. The steps I have outlined won't make the process simple, but I can guarantee that it does get easier with time.

This is why the truly dedicated teachers are so happily exhausted when they go home at night!

~

Would you like even more information on lesson planning, including full-color illustrations? Then check out my other PDF book: *Organizing for the Common Core Part 2: The Visual Guide to Lesson Planning and Student Success.* You can find a link to it on the free resources page: www.ClassroomCaboodle.com/NewTeacher. Whether your state uses Common Core or not, you'll find it to be filled with tons of helpful guidance that you can put to use right away.

Setting up Subs for Success

You never know what will happen when a substitute teacher takes over your classroom. Sometimes substitutes are very effective and can handle any task set before them so the children don't lose a day of progress. Other times... not so much. All you can do is set up your substitute teacher for success as well as you can, understanding that your children may - sometimes - have a day when they sort of tread water academically.

Let me say right here, as a teacher who has subbed, that subbing is very hard work. Not just "every day a new room," but "every day a new room where the classroom teacher has not left you much to work with." So no sub-bashing; understand that guest teachers are from the same pool of people who are classroom teachers, and do your best to make them successful with your kids.

Subbing Scenarios

In an ideal situation, you will get to know the pool of available subs and over time can request one that you know will work well in your room. These are the kinds of substitutes who will be able to take your dollar-store tub full of lesson plans and deliver them almost as well as you would have. This is not something you should expect, however; if your lesson plans are filled with technology, it's going to be the rare sub who can seamlessly integrate interactive whiteboard activities and videos with the same ease and panache that you do.

In a less-than-ideal situation, you will have to call in a sub at the very last minute due to illness or another emergency and will be barely able to provide any direction at all. At the most, you may be able to leave a message with your school office manager about the location of your lesson plans or some other important event (such as the culmination of a project) that is occurring on the day of your absence. Then, you just cross your fingers and hope for the best.

So, what's a teacher to do? How do you do your best to ensure that your kids and your substitute teacher have a good day when you're gone?

The Basic Sub Packet

The key is to do a reasonable amount of preparation and then trust in the fact that guest teachers are certificated and should be able to fill in any gaps that you have left unexplained. Basic preparation means, at a minimum, a substitute teacher package that includes:

- Your daily schedule so that she knows when she is supposed to be teaching different subjects, as well as when lunch, recess, and specialist classes (e.g. fitness) occur.

- Your building's calendar so she knows if there are any school-wide events occurring, such as assemblies.

- The fire drill procedure and her role in it, if it goes beyond shepherding the students.

- How pull-outs work, such as Special Education or gifted-and-talented programs.

- Any special-needs considerations that she should be aware of for particular students.

And that's about it. These are the fundamentals that a substitute teacher will need in order to survive in your classroom for a day without chaos. But what about the actual teaching? Here we must address the two different scenarios mentioned above: when you can plan in advance and when you're out with virtually no notice.

Sub Planning: Advance Notice

As noted, if you are certain your sub can handle it, then she can dive into your tub of lesson plans and get going. However, in all reality, it will be much more common that you can't rely upon a guest teacher to deliver your lessons as you have intended. In that case, you will need to prep something.

In these scenarios, you won't have to create special lesson plans for everything. Instead, you'll probably have to find review activities for certain subject areas, such as math, while letting the sub know the current status in other topics. For example, she may be able to let the kids finish a social studies project that they have already begun, or continue with a rough draft on a writing project.

With a little bit of thought and some trust in the abilities of your guest teacher, prepping for one to three days away should not be that onerous.

Sub Planning: No Notice

And now, about the scenario in which you must be gone with no notice. If you've been keeping the basics that I've outlined above (such as the schedules) in your sub packet, then at least the teacher will not be absolutely lost. Your hasty message to your office manager will let the sub know if there are uncompleted projects to work on or a spelling test to deliver.

However, to ensure that your kids truly have a productive day, you will need to have some "emergency" supplies ready. It's impossible to have a single, set-it-and-forget-it sub packet that is appropriate all year long - you know, a magical packet that you prepare before school begins that will serve for the entire year. If you want your kids to make progress, then you will need to be constantly updating your sub packet with different math worksheets, etc., throughout the year so that, if they must have a review day due to your absence, they are at least reviewing items you have recently taught.

When you are prepping your lesson plans, don't hesitate to throw an extra master of a few worksheets in reading and math into your sub packet. And then, when you do your next planning session, swap them out, whether they have been used or not.

It's also a good idea to include a read-aloud book. Every elementary teacher loves to do a read-aloud, and your sub will be very happy to know that you provided a book the kids have not heard before, but which you know they will like.

Is this a perfect packet? Nope. But it's good enough to keep your students' learning moving forward in your absence, and, frankly, it's all you can realistically expect yourself to manage. If you do this, you will be head and shoulders above 90% of all teachers - and a favorite among your local guest teachers!

Setting Guest Teacher Expectations

Speaking of "being a favorite," you can really build up your reputation among the pool of subs by taking time to set student expectations for how to behave when a guest teacher is in your room. You can imagine what needs to be reinforced:

- Treat a guest teacher with the same respect that they would treat you, their regular teacher

- Be helpful if she has questions about scheduling or classroom procedures

- Be super-polite

Remember, kids perform best if they know they will get your approval; let them know that you love to get compliments on their behavior from substitute teachers and that you can't wait to hear how great they were to teach.

~

It's never a perfect situation when a guest teacher must take over your room. But you can undertake some basic steps to better ensure their success and to put your mind at ease when you must leave your students in another teacher's care.

PART 5

From Zero to Awesome in Record Time

Great teachers do what other teachers won't… and that makes all the difference.

~ *Betsy Weigle*

Supercharging Your Experience

How long does it take to become one of the remembered-by-children-for-the-rest-of-their-lives teachers? Well, that answer depends entirely upon you! I hope to give you a head start with this book, but the progress you make over your first few years of teaching will come from your own efforts.

It's very common to feel uncertain when you start a new job, especially if that job includes managing the needs of twenty to thirty children. When you have that much responsibility, it's natural to want to play it safe and not venture far outside of your classroom comfort zone. In this section, I'm going to make a case for resisting those safety urges and engaging in all the development opportunities available to you within your school. It doesn't take much extra effort - you just have to take full advantage of opportunities that already exist.

The payoff will be a much faster transition from "brand-new" to "been there, seen it, done it." Like everything, experience makes you better. Experienced teachers are simply better for student development. The faster you can become one of those experienced teachers, the better off your kids will be from spending a school year with you as their leader and mentor.

Student-teachers: This Means You!

Please don't think that just because you are spending only a couple of months in a school during your practicum that these tips don't apply to you. I've had experiences with dozens of student-teachers, both in my classroom and in my co-workers' classrooms. It's amazing how the progress of these college students can differ during their time in an elementary school... and it's based entirely upon their attitude and approach to the opportunities presented during their practicum.

A common issue is for a student-teacher to completely imprint upon their mentor teacher. In some cases, this can be ideal. Other times, not so much, if you recall my earlier chapter on the types of mentors you may receive. In reality, even if there is a lot to be learned from your assigned mentor teacher, you should be imprinting upon the *entire* school experience, not only what you can learn from a single person.

It is also quite common to see student-teachers timidly existing on the fringes of the school experience, only stepping to the front when required by their college curriculum. Let me tell you: if you want to be an amazing, child-centered teacher, then your first steps to that exalted status begin when you first set foot in any school during your practicum.

And with that, let's take a look at the experience of "Miss Franklin," a true story with some lessons for both student-teachers and first-year teachers starting a new job.

Being "Miss Franklin"

Question: How does a student-teacher squeeze every last drop of opportunity from their in-classroom, practicum experience?

Answer: With a lot of hustle and a willingness to network with everyone in the school!

I've known of student-teachers who spent the minimum necessary time in the school, and barely any staff even knew they existed. And then others... well, let me share a story.

When my own son was in the middle of his fourth-grade year, we started to hear all about "Miss Franklin." Who was she? He had no idea, just that she was an energetic new teacher that all the kids wanted to know. It turned out that she was a student-teacher for a whole different grade level!

But she actively sought out kids from the entire school. She volunteered to help in other rooms, doing one-on-one work, proctoring tests, giving reading assessments, etc. She went out to the playground once in a while and played with the kids. She even spent time in the lunchroom, engaging with all classes. And she approached parents at pick-up and drop-off time and talked to them about their children.

Within a month or two, every kid knew her, and, as a consequence, every teacher did, too. Why? Because she became the adult with whom children *wanted* to engage.

Recall from our earlier discussions about becoming a classroom leader that elementary children really want to engage with interesting adults. If you demonstrate that you are that kind of adult, the rest will take care of itself.

Are You Hoping for Full-time Work Soon after You Graduate?

I could just as easily have titled this section "How to be a Standout Student-Teacher, Get Noticed, and Get a Job."

The key is to place yourself into situations, as often as possible, where the maximum number of teachers and administrators can experience your approach to teaching and/or interacting with children. How? By reaching out to children in any way you can. I have no doubt that Miss Franklin got sterling recommendations that took her from an "unknown" to a "somewhat-known" quantity when she began her job search. And think of all the child-centered examples she could share during her teacher interviews! Every little bit helps.

Getting Started

What's that? You don't feel like you are ready to jump in and be a "Miss Franklin" right off the bat? Let's start with a baby step. I have an assignment for you.

Any time you walk into a school and check in with the office, whether it's during student teaching, interviewing for a job, or starting your first job, I want you to talk to the first child you see. I'm very serious about this - the very first one, whether she's in the lunchroom or walking down the hall. It doesn't have to be an in-depth conversation. You just have to say, "Where are you headed to?" Say it with a smile and a look of interest on your face, and you are guaranteed to get an answer. If it's a little one, squat down a bit to get on her level.

After she answers, give her a positive affirmation and send her on her way. Simple. But important.

Why am I asking you do this? Because I want you to act like a teacher from the very moment you set foot in any school. And teachers never hesitate to talk to children. I know it can be overwhelming to step into an elementary school when you've been out of grade school for so many years. All the elements that come together to make an elementary school what it is (the sights and sounds and smells and bells and routines) can give you a false impression that it is a carefully balanced system, and that if you interrupt it in any way, you'll be upsetting some critical process. As an "outsider," you may have the feeling that you should sort of drift through unnoticed - and definitely not talk to the young inhabitants of this unique environment.

I'm here to tell you that this veneer of organization that you see in an elementary school is just that: a veneer. Of course there are systems and schedules and things going on, but it's a turbulent place because it is filled with a few hundred young children. The people that keep this system going through constant guidance and corrections are the adults. Therefore, it is no issue whatsoever for you (just another adult) to talk to one of these kids.

Again: teachers talk to children. And you, whether you feel like it or not, are now a teacher - even if you still need to get a piece of paper to certify that.

Jumping In

So you are talking to kids without issue, filling the role they expect of an adult. Next step: jump in.

Student-teachers

Jumping in is particularly necessary for student-teachers. This is your golden opportunity to learn *a lot* during a time when your whole purpose (college) is to learn. So here's your game plan: do anything and everything. This is not the time to show up at 8:59 AM and leave at 3:01 PM. If you really want to be a teacher, you should be mining it for all it's worth:

- Take on the after-school science club.
- Coach the volleyball team.
- Help out at math or reading night.
- Attend staff meetings.
- Attend parent association meetings.

You get the point. Many of these activities will qualify as resume experience - important for someone who doesn't have any paid teaching positions to list.

Remember:

- Observe
- Take notes
- Ask questions

... and do the items listed below as well.

First-time Teachers

While focusing on getting started in your own classroom, you won't have a ton of time for too many extra activities. But you can still make an effort to:

- Go out to recess once a week.

- Sit with your class at lunch once in a while.

- Sit through an entire session of each of the specialist classes (music, fitness, art, etc.).

Be "out and about" and make it a point to get to know kids in other grade levels. You'll be surprised to find the number of parents who request you for their student the following year... even kids you don't recall ever talking to. Congratulations! You've become a local celebrity!

Speaking Up

"Professional courage."

I love that phrase because it describes something that is in great need among the teachers of today. I'm including it in this section because when you start getting super-involved with kids, you'll start noticing inequities right away. As I've mentioned before, "the system" is not always primarily about children. But *teachers* always are. Therefore, sometimes teachers have to show professional courage – even when it's very difficult to do so – on behalf of students. In short, they need to speak up.

I'm not talking about trying to take down the entire testing system because you think it's unfair, or protesting the implementation of standards-based grading. My focus, as always, is on the students. I'm talking about standing up for an individual child who is not being well-treated by the education system. This may include such things as:

- Not getting necessary (or required) services
- Delays in getting services
- Unfair testing scenarios for making up an absence
- Unfair discipline for playground incidents
- Bullying and harassment not noticed by other adults

… and many more. Here's why it's hard: you will likely be treading on someone else's turf when you push things like this. And that is hard to do, especially when the other person is more experienced, more established, or holds a position of higher authority.

Be tactful. Be polite. But, child-focused teacher that you are, be relentless. I have learned over and over again that the persistent person wins, every time. And when you make professional courage part of your image, you'll ultimately gain the respect of your peers.

Student teaching? Use your judgment; you don't have standing to speak up on many issues, and you may not know the entire story, but you can always ask questions. Soon enough, you will be in a position to show plenty of courage.

Expanding Your Role

In an earlier chapter, I talked about "taking center stage" and encouraged you to put on the teacher persona that the children expect you to fill when you walk into their classroom. Acting like the teacher they expect will soon lead to you being the teacher that you hope to become. Now I want you to expand that beyond an individual classroom to the entire school and all the staff.

When you get out of your car in the parking lot of a school, no matter how much confidence you lack, step into your up-and-coming teacher role. Be the person who is not afraid to learn about everything a school has to offer.

So, how do you gain access to all of this information and these experiences? It's actually pretty simple:

- Smile.
- Be friendly.
- Ask questions.
- Be helpful.

You see, *all* people (including you and I) like to talk to people who are interested in them. Of course, you'll run across a few grumps who can't be bothered, but don't worry about it. Just smile, thank them, and move on.

Got the attitude? Great! Let's get into a few details about the people you need to make an effort to meet.

Making School Connections

In the last chapter, I talked about interacting with other people in your school building in order to learn all you can. Now let's get into some of the details. But first, let me emphasize how important this is... not only for you, but also for your students.

Some people may debate whether or not it takes a village to raise a child, but there is no question that it takes an entire school to raise a student. You will, individually, have a tremendous influence on the kids in your care. But they will also be dramatically affected by the other professionals surrounding you. I've always felt that it was my job to help facilitate those relationships in the best interests of my students.

I have found over and over again that other adults in any school where I have taught - from other classroom teachers to music teachers to lunch workers - have given my kids special consideration because they value their relationship with me. Teachers who really care do their best to ensure that their kids have a great experience at school, no matter what activity they are involved in.

Every school job counts. It really does. And you want to be one of the teachers who shows respect and admiration for the jobs done by all of the staff members in your school. Let's cover a few of these critical jobs; it's important to know not only know who they are, but what they do.

~

Student-teachers on practicum: don't skip the ideas in this chapter! Remember "Miss Franklin" - you can never go wrong by introducing yourself and asking questions of any staff member you meet. The more you know about how a school works, the more prepared you'll be when you start your first job.

Your Principal

No kidding, right? But based on how I see most teachers tippy-toeing around their principals, I need to encourage you to interact. You'll interact with your principal to some extent whether you want to or not, of course, but there are far too many teachers who only speak one-on-one with their principal in situations involving stress: evaluations, student misbehavior, parent complaints, etc. Worse, there are teachers whose only private, closed-door conversations with their principals are when a breaking point of some sort has been reached and tears are flowing.

Talk about a negative association! A principal who interacts with you only when stress levels are high may rarely see you at your child-mentoring best.

So cultivate your teacher/principal relationship just as you would any staff relationship. Here's a secret about principals that will make this task easier: their jobs kind of suck. Why? Because they are filled with paperwork, meetings, and constant conflict. This is an ideal opening for you to provide the kinds of positive interactions they'd love to have but don't often get. You can:

- Send a struggling Special Education student who did great on a test down to the office to show the principal his score. Kids really love this, and principals appreciate being able to congratulate individual students for making progress.

- Invite the principal to speak to your class briefly. Principals particularly love to do this if you can somehow tie in your school's character education program, which they always love to talk about. Big bonus points! And - due to your expectation-setting - you get to show off how nicely your class treats visitors.

- Pop in to share your excitement over your class's improvement in reading or math scores. Principals love it when teachers get excited about teaching, since they deal with so many who don't.

- And finally: say "hi" whenever you are in the office. Simple, but so often overlooked.

What's the common thread here? You are not asking the principal to do anything difficult that requires preparation;

you are simply providing purely positive interactions. This is the kind of relationship you want to have before you start those heavy discussions about classroom observations and assessments (covered a bit later).

Office Staff

The staff in the front office are the ones who make it all happen - and believe me, they can make your life in school much easier. I know this firsthand because I worked in a school front office before getting my teaching degree. There are teachers who respect and appreciate the people who do the front-office administration, and those who treat these critical support workers as if they are minions of some sort. Do NOT be one of those teachers!

At your first opportunity, introduce yourself to the office staff and ask what you need to know in order to make their jobs easier. This is not just an idle conversation starter; there are definite ways that attendance can be turned in or the lunch count can be taken that make it easier or harder for them to do their jobs. From your perspective, it doesn't really matter what the procedure is, but from their perspective, it does.

After that, be certain to stop by every single day with something pleasant to say when you check your mailbox. And if you want super bonus points, you can even go above and beyond every once in a while. I have never hesitated to answer a ringing phone in the office and take a message when the staff was swamped with other calls or parents crowding the front counter. Doing something as simple as taking a telephone message will separate you from the vast majority of teachers who can't be bothered.

And who do you think spends all day in close proximity to the office staff? Yep, your principal. If you make an effort with them, they will naturally end up promoting you to their boss.

Tip: Don't forget the office staff on the gift-giving holidays!

Other Support Staff

Custodial Staff

Find your custodians and introduce yourself within the first couple of days of arriving at school. There will usually be daytime custodians and those who work at night cleaning rooms. Want to score some points? Ask their preferences regarding how you tidy up your room at night in order to make the cleaning job easier. And while you're at it, you can confirm where to empty the garbage and recycle bins in your classroom.

Always thank them for the work they do, and teach your students to thank them as well.

Lunchroom Staff and Aides

You can help avoid the tangle of confusion that occurs in the lunchroom during the first week of school if you take some time to ask questions of the lunchroom staff. It's quite common for teachers to dump their children at the entrance to the lunchroom and head off to their own free time. The staff will really appreciate it, however, if you not only understand their procedures, but also take time to set expectations and reinforce processes with your class before dropping them off at the lunchroom.

As with the custodians, teach your students to thank the lunchroom staff daily.

By the way, your children will love having you eat with them in the lunchroom at least a couple times a month. My kids know that I love tater tots and that, on tater-tot day, I will eat with them. On many occasions, a breathless student has burst into my room, having run back from the lunchroom to inform me that it was tater-tot day. I always take a few minutes to go down, buy some tater tots, and eat them sitting with my class.

Great memories!

Recess Aides

You will find, during your time as an elementary teacher, that there are many behavior issues that will spill over from recess into your room. Behavior on the playground can be a very difficult thing to manage, so it's good to make allies of the recess aides so that you can get their observations to offset the "he said/she said" testimony from your kids.

The first time your students are sent out to recess, go with them and introduce yourself to the aides. Ask them to give you a quick tour of the playground to help you understand the activities that are allowed and those that are forbidden. During this conversation, you'll get a sense of how effective they are at their jobs, which will give you the appropriate context when trying to sort out contradicting claims of misbehavior and unfairness.

Classroom Aides (or Paraprofessionals)

You may or may not qualify for classroom assistance. If you do, obviously, you'll get to know your assigned paraprofessional quickly. But, even if you don't, you never know when you will be working one-on one with the classroom aides, such as when they are helping to proctor tests. Be certain to say "hi" and introduce yourself at your first opportunity and ask about their jobs.

Art, Music, Library, and Fitness

Far too many teachers treat specialist classes like they do the lunchroom: leave the kids at the door and walk away until it's time to pick them up again. Yes, of course the art, library, music, and fitness teachers are trained professionals just like you and don't need handholding. But failing to introduce yourself and participate to a certain extent with your class in these specialist sessions is leaving a huge learning opportunity on the table. Let me explain.

Remember, kids learn best when they are engaged. And engagement does not have to occur only during your lessons; standards-based engagement can occur even when the children are not in your room. Your specialists will have a specific curriculum they are teaching, but I have always found them to be more than willing to work with me to reinforce content that I am teaching in the classroom. For example:

- Art projects that incorporate geometric designs or other math concepts

- Musical numbers that dovetail with social studies curriculum

- Library research that is aligned with informational essays in writing

Fitness can be harder to align with your classroom curriculum, but innovative collaboration can often find a way.

You will immediately stand out as an exceptional classroom teacher with the specialists if you do nothing more than spend a few extra minutes after dropping off your kids to ensure that they are settled, and showing up one or two minutes early to pick them up. It's so easy – and fun – to have time to "ooh" and "aah" over the artwork that has been created, or hear the final rendition of the song your students have been practicing for the last thirty minutes. You can also hear first-hand if there have been any behavior issues that may need to be worked on as a team.

Like in the lunchroom, there are definite procedures that need to be followed in the specialist classrooms; you can help set expectations around these procedures. Believe me, the specialists will appreciate it!

Special Education

I love, love, love my Special Education students. These kids really need all the resources that a school can provide, so coordination with the SPED teachers is super important for the success of your children.

Find out who the Special Education teachers are right away and seek them out to ask about how they administer the IEP's in the building. Also, there will be some combination of delivery of their services to the children in your classroom or (more commonly) pulling children out. You'll want to ask how you can coordinate the work that is being done in your room with the Special Education teachers so that they can help support students in performing grade-level tasks.

Please, *please* do not hand off responsibility for the success of your Special Ed students or the fulfillment of their IEP's completely to the Special Education staff! I have always considered the primary responsibility of fulfilling an IEP to be mine because the kids spend a lot more time with me than they do in Special Education. If they are going to make progress and exit their IEP's, then I know that I must be working with them constantly on the necessary skills.

Regardless, Special Education provides critical individualized support, so you want to remain closely coordinated with these specialists.

Other Grade Levels

Find some time within the first month of being in a school (whether you are student-teaching or starting a new job) to introduce yourself to every other teacher in the building, whether they are in your grade level or not. In the big picture, you will be getting students from some of these teachers and passing your students on to others, so it's good to know all of them.

Some schools have programs that pair up different grade levels for "buddy" time. It would be nice to know the names of the teachers with whom you feel you are most compatible if there is any chance to influence these assignments when they are made.

Collaboration

Nearly every school will have a formalized collaboration program in place. Oftentimes, this will rotate between whole-group collaboration and grade-level collaboration. The point, of course, is to ensure that teachers are being consistent in how they are teaching curriculum from one grade level to the next or among the same grade level.

By the way, it is during your first whole-group collaboration that you will be happy you introduced yourself to the other grade levels in your building! It makes it so much easier when you're broken down into small groups if you already have an acquaintance with the other professional staff.

Frankly, sometimes collaborations are effective, and sometimes they are not. And (also frankly), it's usually the person with whom you are collaborating that will make the difference. Some teachers simply don't do well in this area and put up roadblocks to effectively getting anything done. Don't be one of those teachers.

You don't have all the answers, so always be willing to learn from others - that's the main attitude for collaborative success. Be prepared, be humble, listen, ask questions. You may or may not apply all that you learn, but fresh perspectives are always welcome.

Partnering with Parents

Parent-teacher communication is absolutely critical for creating the best possible education environment for kids. You might think this statement seems kind of obvious, but I have found that many teachers are so nervous about communicating with parents that they avoid it completely unless they absolutely must deal with an issue.

You - being the dedicated teacher that you are - won't make this mistake! Parent partnerships are critical for your success. Let's review some of the reasons that teachers often have difficulty embracing this fact.

Communication Roadblocks

What emotions and mindsets stand in the way of effective parent outreach?

Fear

Many people experience trepidation when calling a stranger whom they fear may judge them. It's the same reason that you don't like calling an authority figure, such as an attorney or doctor. What many teachers don't realize is that parents - even the parents of the well-behaved children - fear *teachers*. More on that in a bit.

Be the first to break down this barrier. Your parent-teacher communication motto: No Fear.

Assumptions

Many teachers assume that some of their students' parents just don't care about school. In some instances, they are right, but it is the rare parent who has no interest whatsoever. The only assumption you should be making about parents is that they are critical for your students' success.

Disdain

Repeated exposure to parents who don't care much about school can leave teachers with a "seen-this-situation-before" attitude. This attitude will slowly poison a critical relationship. Restart your willingness to interact with parents at the beginning of every new year; you'll always find at least a few who welcome the engagement when you provide the opening.

Parent involvement will vary, depending upon the school's constituency. There are schools that are overflowing with parent volunteers, and it is easier to form relationships with your kids' primary mentors. Other schools have no parent involvement at all, and parent-teacher communication can be very hard to get started.

Parent Involvement: The Reality

In case you have an overly optimistic assessment of your powers of persuasion, I'd like to clarify something right now: never go into any conversation with a parent, thinking that you'll be able to say something that gets them to magically transform their child's behavior in school. It won't happen, at least not to the extent you hope. It may not even happen if you are meeting with them to fill out a behavior contract.

Parents influence school behavior, but teachers control it. The days are long, long gone when a child who got into trouble at school got into twice as much trouble at home. So let's move on.

Don't Blame Parents

Blaming the parents should not be your instinctive first response when a behavior problem arises with a child. This is not an effective teaching strategy, nor a teaching practice that will lead to truly making a difference in the life of a student. I'm not talking about negligent parents here, the ones who don't fulfill the basic health and safety obligations of child-rearing that our society expects. I'm talking about your standard, do-your-best-but-not-perfect parents. (I'm including my own imperfect parenting here.)

No matter how conscientious a parent is, they cannot completely prepare their child to perform like a perfect little teacher-pleasing robot at school. Even if this is what the system required (which it doesn't), what parent can fully prepare their child to handle this new and ever-changing dynamic that we call "school"?

School is a lot of things - constant interaction with dozens of kids of all different personalities, plus rules, rituals, rewards, consequences, procedures, and new stuff - that stretches students' brains to the limit every day. And what about recent immigrants to this country who may not even speak English at home? They are even less well-equipped to prepare their children for the social expectations of an American school.

All a "good" parent can really do is send their kid through the doors of the school every day as well-prepared as they can make them, then pick them up six hours later and do their best to get them ready to repeat it all again the next day. If a little reinforcement of learning can happen at home, that's a great bonus.

In between drop-off and pick-up, during those six hours when a child is outside the direct influence of his parents, that's when the trained, experienced professional takes over. You know, the one who has learned effective teaching strategies, has a college degree (often a Master's), and plenty of resources in the form of a full professional support staff, not to mention experienced colleagues - the one who has made it her life's work to develop children into knowledgeable, intelligent citizens.

So I have a bit of a problem when the first reaction of a trained, professional teacher to a common classroom issue (such as talking during lessons) is to blame the parents. That is an unfortunate and unproductive attitude for any teacher to hold.

By the way, we are never going back to the days when kids were taught to automatically respect all authority figures. It's a different society now - one in which authority figures must earn respect.

Here's the thing: every child deserves a great teacher. If we hold every parent to an unrealistic and unattainable standard of child-rearing, and only want to teach the "good" kids, we are excluding those children who need us, and who need the benefits of education the most. If there is one profession that demands dedication, teaching is it. And when it comes to dedication, I mean dedication to children with all of their unique, engaging, aggravating, irritating, and inspiring little personalities.

That's simply what being a teacher is all about.

Building Parent Relationships

You want to have relationships with your students' parents *before* you need to contact them about problems; it makes these discussions *so* much easier. My advice? Make the first move.

The onus is on you to reach out and create a safe and welcoming environment that encourages parent involvement. Why? Because many parents fear interaction with you, as I mentioned before. Yep… whether you feel like it or not, you represent an authority figure - an authority figure who may have been experiencing their child at her worst behavior. I clearly remember waiting nervously in the hall with my husband to meet my son's second-grade teacher. This was before I went back to college for my teaching degree, and the school seemed to be absolutely *filled* with authority figures who were judging me as a parent.

Parents are people, and people fear and dislike being judged. Our goal is to create a parent-teacher relationship that could be described as "professional friendship." Here's how.

Teach With Total Transparency

There is nothing secret going on in your classroom, ever. Just as your principal can drop by at any time, so can parents. Let them know this, even if what they are stopping by to see is your management of their own child.

Search For Parent-teacher Communication Opportunities

Go to where the parents are:

- The bus line
- The drop-off/pick-up location
- The volunteer luncheon
- The after-school bingo night

Ask For Input

I like to assign homework for parents to complete on the first day of school:

> "What do you want me to know about your child?"

Kids love giving their parents homework to do on the first day, and parents really appreciate this outreach. It's simple to do and has a high impact on your parent-teacher relationship. It's a good time to collect email addresses, too.

Be A Little Extroverted

I've talked about being a bit of an extrovert with the kids; the same holds true with their parents. As I said above, "make the first move." If you don't, you will remain strangers to your kids' parents for far too long. Approach parents, greet them, learn their names, and use them. And use their child's name when talking to them; this lets them know that you have a caring relationship with their student.

Address Their Biggest Concern Up Front

A parent's biggest concern is easy to predict: "How is Janelle doing in class?" That's all they really care about. So tell them; don't make them ask.

But, just like you don't want to hear a list of horrible behaviors from your substitute teacher, parents don't want a load of bad news every time they see you - that would be another one of those negative associations! Parents know how challenging their child can be - what they are looking for is a ray of hope that he has some redeeming qualities and that you recognize them and celebrate them.

Compliment their child in a specific manner every time you talk to them, especially if their child is listening.

> "Ray put in super effort on the spelling test today."

> "Today, Andrea gave a classmate the nicest compliment that I've ever heard!"

Cementing Parent Relationships

Usually parents operate on the "no news is good news" principle when it comes to their kids' behavior and parent-teacher communication. If the school phones, most parents are going to assume it is bad news.

So surprise them: call or email to let them know that their child demonstrated some great behavior.

Picture being a parent and how you would feel if your kid's teacher called to let you know how kind your child was to another child in school. Your child, your pride and joy, doing good things *and* being acknowledged for them. "Geez," you'd think, "Maybe I'm not such a bad parent, after all!"

Yes, assuaging parental worry/guilt is an acceptable relationship-building technique! I can tell you that I never got communication like this from any of my kids' teachers, ever. But when I make these calls, I can feel the pride and relief of the parents flowing through the phone line.

It's hard to make time for this, but it's important. And I don't care if you suspect the parent had no role in mentoring their child to achieve this great behavior - tell them, anyway. Build that relationship.

Here's one more positive excuse to contact parents: to thank them if they send any supplies to the classroom.

Parent Communication

A regular newsletter is a good idea, but not critical for keeping parents informed - mainly because getting parents to read it is way harder than you may think. You can give your newsletter a better chance of being read by consistently using the same color paper so it stands out in the disorganized wad of papers that tumble out of backpacks after school.

"Ah," you may be thinking, "then a class website would be a better solution for these tech-savvy parents." If your school provides easy tools for creating and maintaining web pages, then go for it. But again, check your stats - you'll likely find that visitors are rare.

So what's the most effective way to get the word out? Email. Gather those addresses early on in the year and send out short, concise emails every week or two with pertinent things parents need to know. Attach PDF permission slips to be printed, signed, and returned. If you have more info on your web page, include a link, but the main points should be in the email.

Tip: If you are being super-efficient, save a copy of the text from every email on a Word document. This will save you from having to come up with a way to describe the same annual event (such as the fall festival) every single year.

~

So we have a great relationship established with our students' parents. Now it's time to see how that relationship stands up when it's tested!

Parents and Discipline

The parent-teacher relationship can withstand conversations about poor behavior *if* we use the right tone of voice and phrases. Here are the six keys to getting through a difficult discussion with Mom or Dad:

1. Start the conversation with a friendly greeting.
2. Stay focused on the issue at hand.
3. Be gentle and speak with a calm voice.
4. Step into the parent's shoes and consider what they are hearing.
5. Present a positive along with the negative.
6. Provide a task for the parent to complete.

Let's walk through a scenario.

Six Steps That Preserve Relationships

What happened: Reuben was verbally bullying another boy, making fun of his speech impediment until the victim cried. This is some very tough news to deliver to a parent! But we can do it with professionalism and empathy.

1. Start the Conversation with a Friendly Greeting

> "Hi, Mrs. Thomason, this is Sharon Smith, Reuben's teacher. Did I catch you at a good time to talk?"

Allow the parent to respond before rushing into your reason for calling. Be the calm professional and let Mom absorb the fact that the teacher is calling (which normally is not a good thing). Then continue with a "we're in this together" statement before she even hears the bad news:

> "I need to share with you what happened with Reuben today and to let you know how you can help out."

2. Stay Focused on the Issue At Hand

Provide a succinct statement about everything that occurred. She needs to know the full extent of the incident.

> "Reuben was making fun of another boy's lisp today, and it went on for a while. The other boy finally let me know about it after lunch recess, and Reuben did spend some time in the principal's office."

Caution: What does human nature compel us to do when we are trying to sell someone on our point of view? We pile on the reasons, trying to build an assault-proof structure that will stand against any attack. DO NOT DO THIS.

3. Be Gentle and Speak with a Calm Voice

Always remember that you are talking about a child. Sometimes, in our frustration over behavior and our trepidation about calling parents, this is easy to forget, and we act like we are an attorney delivering closing arguments to convince a jury of a defendant's guilt. Tap very, very lightly. Do not get out the metaphorical sledgehammer and pound on your point, even if you are staying focused on the pertinent issue.

Humans feel the blows of criticism with enhanced sensitivity. Think of your own reaction to anyone – even your best friend – criticizing anything about you. Whether it is your choice of shoes or your choice of spouses, criticism is very hard to take. Now, imagine your reaction to an authority figure criticizing you - it's ten times worse to get pointed comments from your boss than gentle comments from a close friend.

So don't get all psyched up for a call and start delivering knock-out punches. The teacher-parent relationship will not survive such an approach. You need only a couple of concise points, spoken gently, in order for most parents to feel like they are receiving a body blow.

But, just because you are being gentle doesn't mean you shouldn't name what happened.

> "We had a serious discussion about what bullying is and how it affects other children."

Notice that the word "bullying" is surround by an assurance that we had a discussion, not a lecture.

4. Step Into the Parent's Shoes and Consider What They are Hearing

Put yourself in the place of Mom or Dad. If a teacher calls to complain about your child's behavior, what do you actually hear? Do you hear:

> "Ms. Jones, Lance made some poor choices at lunch today and hit another student."

Or do you hear:

> "Ms. Jones, I think you are a horrible parent."

When I got a call from preschool about my son knocking over other kids' blocks (I'm not kidding – this really happened!), it caused me to question my entire mothering ability. "But I'm a stay-at-home mom!" I said to my husband. "This isn't supposed to happen! What have I done wrong?"

Unless the parents are completely jaded to their kid's poor behavior (and plenty of these parents exist), Mom and Dad will feel at least a bit of guilt and self-recrimination over poor school behavior. We can't stop that from happening, but we do want to keep them on our team for the benefit of the student. Stopping for questions is a good way to insert a natural breathing space into your delivery so that you aren't doing all of the talking (it's a discussion, not a lecture... just like you had with Reuben).

> "Do you have any questions I can answer about what happened?"

Keep answers short and factual. Examples:

> Mom: "Oh my gosh... I'm so sorry."

264

You: "I know. I wanted you to have all of the information so you could talk to Reuben tonight."

Mom: "How do you know he really did it?"

You: "The playground aide saw and heard it happening, and then Reuben admitted it."

5. Provide a Positive along with the Negative

Think about this in advance so you are ready. As much as parents may agonize over their child's behavior, they will also instinctively want to protect them from unfairness. Including a positive statement lets parents know that you have not permanently labeled Reuben as a behavior problem and that you will continue to engage with him fairly and constructively.

> "So Reuben didn't meet my expectations about working with others in our community, but the good news is that he was very honest about what he did, and I could tell that he understood how it made the other boy feel."

6. Provide a Task for the Parents to Complete

This is a very important step for showing the parents that you are all on the same team and that they can help you manage the behavior so it has less chance of occurring in the future. Be specific.

Remember, don't assume that any discussion will cause parents to "fix" their student's behavior; that's not the point of providing this task. The point is - again - maintaining that all-important teacher-parent relationship. Asking the parents to do something for you confirms that they are a valued member of the classroom team.

> "It would be really helpful to have Reuben write a short apology note. Consider it part of his homework tonight."

Another Example

What happened: Taneeka has been cheating on her tests, copying from others.

> "Good afternoon, Mr. Addington. This is Sharon Smith, calling from school. I hope I caught you at a time when you can talk.

> "Taneeka has been having some difficulty with doing her own work on tests for the last few weeks. It hasn't been too bad, and I've been working with her. But today, she took another student's test from my in-box and copied every answer word-for-word on our reading assessment, and I really thought you should know about it. Here's what happened.

> "I had moved her desk closer to mine a few days ago, but when we had a substitute teacher this morning, she waited until a few students turned in their tests. She asked to get a pencil and took a test out of the in box, copied it, and turned them both in.

> "This afternoon, when I talked to her about it, she tried to tell me that was impossible, but I got to the bottom of what happened pretty quickly.

> "Do you have any questions?

"Taneeka is a smart girl; she's just lacking some confidence that she knows the material. I had Taneeka redo the test during recess, and I think she really learned something from that; she was surprised how much she knew all on her own.

"I would really appreciate it if you could ask Taneeka to talk through the entire event and then ask her what she learned. I think it would reinforce what I'm telling her in class.

"I'm sending home both the test she copied and the one she did on her own, so those should be in her backpack."

Leaving a Message

If you have to leave a message:

"Hello, Ms. Pietro, this is Sharon Smith from school. I would like to talk to you today when you get a chance. Nic had a little trouble at school today, which we've handled, but I wanted you to know about it. You can call me after 3:00 today on my classroom phone at this number..."

Yes, that message may cause a parent to freak out a little, but at least they'll most likely call back!

When to Call

Calling home can reinforce the effect of classroom behavior interventions... if it is not overused. Kids usually don't want Mom and Dad to know they've gotten into trouble, but if we call parents after every little incident, we'll spend every evening on the phone. Aside from losing its impact due to overuse, it's not necessary.

And when it comes to student behavior issues, you really have to *call* - a note or an email is acceptable only if three of your phone messages have been ignored. So, when do you inform parents of something going on at school? Here are some guidelines:

When Your Building Discipline Plan Requires It

Pretty simple: if the plan says to call, then call. Building-wide plans start to unravel if one teacher decides to go her own way.

When a Student Has Interfered with the Safety of Others

Bullying and fighting fit into this category, as does anything else that judgment tells you is bad for student physical or mental health. I once called eighteen sets of parents to advise of both good and bad behavior arising from a significant bullying incident.

When the Principal Should Have Called but Didn't

Many principals tend to avoid conflict when they can. If, in your judgment, parents should be informed of a school behavior issue, then don't let a principal's inaction stop you. Classroom teachers are the ones who have to live with the future actions of a misbehaving student. Make the call.

When the Principal Does Call but Parents also Need to Hear from You

You are the one with the carefully built parent-teacher relationship - a relationship that is usually much more solid than any parent-principal connection. There are times when parents need to hear from their child's classroom teacher so they understand that you are still on their team on behalf of their child.

When a Trend Develops

When a behavior pattern has gone on for an extended period of time, each incident may not warrant a call, but an accumulation leading to a trend does.

When Not to Call

Notice that I didn't say, "Call when a student is sent to the office." Kids are sent to the office for all kinds of things (often unnecessarily), from chewing gum to making knives out of rulers. We don't need to call Mom and Dad about gum-chewing; that kind of "teacher tattling" erodes parent-teacher relationships.

A knife, on the other hand… it's good idea to call on that one!

Teacher-parent relationships must be based on trust. A big part of trust is letting parents know that you don't sound the alarm at every childish transgression; you save the personal communication for important stuff, not trivia.

Teacher Observations and Assessments

Just like testing is a part of education for our students, teacher assessments are an inescapable part of our jobs. This begins, of course, when you are student-teaching and - in today's education system - never ends. Teacher assessments used to be infrequent and carried few consequences; in many parts of the country, the opposite is now the norm.

Understandably, this is upsetting to many teachers. However, for some perspective, I encourage you to talk to your friends who are working for large corporations. You will find that they are assessed even more frequently than teachers and have had to learn to live with the reality that their continued employment can be called into question at any time based on their performance... and union protections are quite rare in cubicle-land.

I'm not saying that it's an ideal situation (after all, elementary education is different from the standard cubicle job) but I am saying that it is inevitable. Therefore, you need to understand how to survive and thrive in this culture of teacher observations and assessments.

As with so many things, it starts with *attitude.*

The Assessment Attitude

You have a choice to make when it comes to teacher evaluations. You can fight against and agonize over them for the rest of your career, or you can learn to live with and even benefit from them without undue stress.

Notice I didn't say you had to "like them."

Nobody likes to be criticized. No matter how skillful an evaluator is in giving feedback, it will still feel like criticism. That's why you are never actually going to like being observed, but you can get to the point where you don't spend sleepless nights with your stomach churning prior to observation days.

How is that accomplished?

Forgive Yourself for Not Being Perfect

Yes, step one is making a decision up front that you are not going to be your own harshest critic, no matter what anybody else says. Everybody makes mistakes. Everybody has trouble implementing the latest and greatest classroom requirement that administration has handed down. Everybody has off days when their children are not on their best behavior and lessons don't go well.

You are going to have to make the decision that you are doing your best and that even though you are always trying to improve, you will never be a perfect teacher. And that is entirely okay; imperfect people change the world all the time, don't they?

Forgive Your Reviewer for Not Being Perfect

This is very important. We are all human, and, just as you are not a perfect teacher, the vast majority of people evaluating you are not perfect at being evaluators. It can be a very difficult skill to learn what to look for and how to document it. But, it can be an almost impossible skill for some people to learn how to deliver feedback in an empathetic and constructive way.

This is so difficult that you can always expect that any time you receive feedback, it will have some sharp and jagged edges that will rub against your psyche in ways that the reviewer does not intend. No matter how angry they are making you at the moment, or how insecure you feel, take a little bit of time to forgive them for not being the greatest at a difficult task.

Accept That You Are Not Perfect

This sounds a little bit like the first one, doesn't it? But it's not. Forgiving yourself for not being perfect is different from accepting that you still have things that you can work on in order to improve as a teacher. During much of our young lives, we are used to being constantly evaluated and criticized, both informally and formally. But, after we enter into our professions, we no longer feel like we are in official "learning" mode, and therefore it's not okay to be imperfect. That's when evaluations begin to sting.

You are in the field of education, so you are going to have to decide that *your* learning will extend for the rest of your career. And, since you are in perpetual learning mode, of course you will be making course adjustments along the way. Getting feedback from observers is a very important part of this... just like your feedback to your students is very important for their improved performance.

Think of it this way: you are setting a good example for your students by reflecting upon constructive criticism and figuring out how to do things better.

Those are the fundamental steps to having the proper attitude about evaluations. But we can do even better by adopting a proactive approach that puts us more in control of the process.

Inviting Assessment

It is very common for teachers to feel like they are targets when being evaluated. I mean, literally feeling like you are standing down at the end of the shooting range and the observer in the back of the classroom is taking dead aim at you. You feel helpless and powerless in the face of a process in which you believe you have no input, and therefore you have no control over the outcome.

That, my teacher friends, is absolutely not true.

If you adopt the attitude of inviting feedback in order to improve (as I have suggested), then you are automatically placing yourself in the position of making evaluations a collaborative process rather than a judgmental one. How?

Ask for Evaluation

This approach applies particularly to student-teachers. There will be a few formal assessments throughout your time in a mentor teacher's classroom, but not nearly as many as you need. In order to truly prepare for your future, you should ask the principal of your building to give you an evaluation of your teaching. I'm not kidding! If you want to know what it's like to be a real teacher, then you need to feel what it's like to be observed by the administration.

But this approach is not only for student-teachers; new teachers can also ask to be evaluated informally sooner rather than later. Instead of waiting around for a few months to get hit with your first assessment (at which point you may complain that you never knew you were supposed to be doing certain things), think of the power you can gain by asking for an informal evaluation up front. You are in learning mode as a new teacher, and this is a golden opportunity to figure out the administration's philosophy and hot buttons before it really counts for anything.

Seriously, all you have to do is go to your principal and say:

> "I'm pretty confident in my math lesson planning and delivery, but I would really appreciate it if you could find fifteen minutes to sit in my classroom and give me an informal assessment of how I'm implementing my mini-lessons."

If your principal doesn't drop dead from shock, she should be happy to accommodate you.

Tip: Notice that you should ask for a *specific* evaluation, not a generalized drop-by-and-check-out-my-teaching session.

Acknowledge Your Weaknesses Up Front

We all know what our weaknesses are in teaching, don't we? Well, assuming that you actually want to get better in these areas, involve your observer in the process.

> "I would really like your feedback on how I'm redirecting a few of my students who have difficulty staying on task during my mini-lessons. So, no matter what else you are looking for, if you could keep an eye on that, I would love to discuss it afterward."

See what you've done? You've demonstrated to your principal that you are actively looking to improve as a professional educator and that you are being honest in your self-assessment. You have also made the post-observation discussion much less threatening because you already know that you're going to be talking about some shortcomings, and you've mentally prepared yourself to accept input. This will soften any other aspects of the observation that are also revealed to you.

... And Keep Acknowledging Them

You can carry this approach through to the next assessment. When you've been given some feedback that you perceived to be negative after an evaluation, it will take you a few days to calm your nerves and be able to think about it objectively. If you arrive at the point where you admit that there could be at least a grain of truth in it, then you'll make a plan to try to improve. Good for you! Now take it to the next step.

Before your next observation, tell your principal what you've been working on and ask him to give you feedback on how you are implementing your improvement plan. Again, this makes the observation much more collaborative, and it will feel less judgmental.

Another huge benefit: It will demonstrate to your administration that you are a teacher who is constantly striving to improve, not a teacher who is constantly resisting improvement. It's never an individual observation or evaluation that will put a judgmental stamp on your teaching career; it's the trend of your assessments. There will be some ups and some downs, but as long as the trend line is moving in the right direction, you will always be fine when it comes to any scoring system that may be in place. Teachers who are constantly striving to improve tend to move the scoring trend in the right direction.

And, human nature being what it is, administrators will be more lenient toward your imperfections if they see you actively working to get better.

Handling the "Latest Thing"

Okay, it's time to loop back around and talk about attitude again. I need to discuss with you how much to fight against some of the feedback that you will receive.

Here's the thing with large organizations, whether they are public schools or private corporations: they all love to roll out new ways of doing things. In large corporations, it's common to go through at least one or two big launches every year of new, theoretically-much-improved processes. Meetings are held, posters are posted, flurries of emails are sent out. Often, of course, these big launches are based upon the latest-and-greatest trend that is sweeping the industry, usually driven by highly-paid consultants.

After a few months or a year, it's very common to walk by these posters, still hanging on the walls, and chuckle because they are starting to be covered up by the *new* new posters for the *latest* latest-and-greatest thing.

Education is no different. Trends sweep through teaching, education consultants circulate in and out of superintendents' offices, and up-and-coming administrators in your district headquarters keep trying to make names for themselves. So, some of the feedback you will receive will center around:

- Not having the prescribed charts and posters or other required teaching aids displayed in the correct manner

- Not using the prescribed words or phrases that are supposed to be the key to unlocking the knowledge of the universe

- Generally not "getting with the program" regarding something that your principal has been told is super-important. She may not personally believe that it is, but she'd really rather keep her job and is not willing to risk it over this particular requirement.

I'm being a little bit snarky here because I've been through so many of these cycles that it's hard not to be!

You are going to have to decide up front that you will go along with these flavor-of-the-month requirements and not get overly concerned about them. Whether you use the posters or not, just put them up if they don't get in the way of great teaching and learning. Don't stress out about it; do what you've been asked and understand that if the latest-and-greatest is something unworkable and even silly, it will pass before too long, and you can trash the unnecessary wall support or drop the silly teaching method. (Don't worry about saving anything; you'll be issued new supplies for the next round, even if it's something that's been tried before.)

But Keep an Open Mind!

Don't be *too* dismissive of these trendy requirements. The vast majority of them don't stick, but every standardized, accepted, best-practice teaching method that is being used in today's classrooms started as a new "thing" at some point. Some do stick. Therefore, you need to give each of them a fair shot and keep an open mind.

The main point here is not to stress about it or fight against it - that approach will make your observations even harder on yourself. Go along and see what happens... all the while taking it with a giant grain of salt.

Video: The Ultimate Assessment

Are you feeling really brave? Then you can supercharge your assessment by asking to be filmed. This will almost always be an informal thing because a principal cannot film you and fill out her observation sheets at the same time. However, with the ubiquity of cell phone cameras, it's no issue at all to have somebody quickly film something that you are doing in the classroom that you want feedback on.

I get it: it is really hard to watch yourself on video. After all, I've put out a couple of hundred YouTube videos, and I still flinch every time I watch myself online! But the camera does reveal a lot. If you are a student-teacher, it is very easy to ask your mentor teacher to film portions of your lessons, or even to film you working one-on-one or with small groups of children.

New classroom teachers can also benefit from this. You can ask an aide, an assistant principal, or even your spouse to film you if they are officially registered with the school and able to be in your classroom. Look for ways to make this happen.

Remember, the person who is filming you is doing only that: filming. They do not need to watch the video with you afterward, and they certainly do not need to offer any critiques. You will do enough of that on your own when you watch yourself!

And here's a final note of caution: Be very aware of your district's policy regarding photographing or filming children. You may not need to take any special precautions if you are not distributing the film and you are deleting it when you are done. Still, there may be a requirement for a media release if the children appear in the film, even if you are not distributing it.

Don't let this stop you, however - I'm not trying to provide you with an excuse for not filming! It's so valuable that you should take the few necessary minutes to research it.

Student-teacher Assessments

I've mentioned student-teachers throughout this chapter, but I want to be certain that you understand the critical importance of assessments during this phase of your career.

Within a few months, you are going to have all kinds of people watching you: students, principals, aides, parent volunteers. At that point, they will all be expecting you to know what you are doing, and your full-time job will be on the line. Student-teacher evaluations will seem easy by comparison!

I want you to take full advantage of this golden phase of your life when you are expected to mess things up. Remember, this is one long interview. Many teachers have gotten their first jobs in the same buildings in which they student-taught. Demonstrate that you are easy to work with and open to feedback.

Self-assessment

Throughout this chapter, I stress the importance of not only being open to input, but also being self-reflective when you are given that input. This doesn't apply only to formal assessments, of course. It is very important to constantly be asking yourself what you can do better so that your children receive the best education possible.

Every teacher I know is constantly questioning herself on a daily basis. Resolve to not only *question* yourself, but to *improve* yourself and act upon the input from the harshest critic in the world: you. You don't want to get on this critic's bad side by failing to make progress! So buckle down and do it.

Falling Down and Getting Up

I tried to come up with a more positive title for this chapter, but in the end, I decided to call it what it is. Learning how to be a standout teacher can be like a journey along a hard and rocky road - especially if you're traveling down that road at a rapid pace (like I keep pushing you to do!). If you play it safe and pick your way around the rocks, you're not likely to experience as many "uh-oh" moments. But if you are doing what's in the best interest of the kids and making progress as quickly as you can, you are going to find yourself tripping over rocks constantly.

This chapter is about giving you some perspective so you can get back up and keep on moving, no matter what happens.

Kids Bounce Back from Teacher Mistakes

I keep saying that it's all about the students, don't I? Well, one of the things you may worry about is that your mistakes are impacting your kids. Yes, to a certain extent they are, but it is a very short-term thing, as long as you are always striving to improve.

A follower once shared something that her college professor asked, which I thought was brilliant. This professor asked:

> "What was the worst thing that ever happened to you in school? Who did it to you?"

If you think about it, the worst thing that ever occurred to most people in elementary school never came from a teacher; it nearly always came from other children. You have to do a lot to scar a child for life, so it is highly unlikely that you are ever going to hurt them or their long-term success if you are teaching with their best interests at heart.

Your Classroom Laboratory

> "First, do no harm."

This is a basic principle that medical doctors take into consideration when dealing with patients. The same principle can be applied to dealing with students. We don't want to do anything that will set them back in any way, either academically or emotionally. However, there is still plenty of experimenting that we can do without harming students in the slightest.

I've encouraged you to do some of these things throughout this book, such as trying read-alouds with boring voices vs. exciting voices, or wearing different outfits to assess their impact on children.

Always be experimenting in all areas of your teaching practice. If you see another teacher doing something that looks effective or even just intriguing, give it a shot, whether it's a method of lining up for lunch or a new approach to diagramming sentences. You're with the children for six or more hours every day, so there is always time to try something new and then correct it if it doesn't work.

Resolve to not be one of those people who is always "planning to try something" but never quite gets around to it. Instead, be a person who immediately tries out new things and then accepts, rejects, or adjusts based on the results. You will make tremendous progress toward your goal of being an outstanding teacher if you are willing to rapidly work your way through all manner of new ways of doing things.

Calling for a "Do-over"

One of my European followers wrote this question to me:

> "I came off to a bad start with a few students in a fourth grade class. They are the class-clowns and like to be troublemakers, and I have a hard time keeping them busy because they don't do the tasks I ask of them. Now, to be a self-critic, I worked with many of the kids in the class before becoming their substitute teacher (in Denmark, the kids go to a daycare kind of thing after school to have fun, that's where I worked), so many of them already knew me really well. I didn't feel the need

to introduce myself, so I simply said my name and got on with it.

"However, I see now that that was a mistake; some of the kids didn't know me at all. Now I want to get onto a fresh start with them... especially the kids who have given me some trouble. Do you have an idea of how I can do that? Seeing as I should be able to handle these things, as I worked with kids their age for half a year and have faced quite a few of their issues, it makes me feel so freaking bad, like I am failing at my job."

And my response:

"Gravin:

"As the adult, you get to call a 'do-over' whenever you want. You only have to state that 'things didn't go well, and we are going to start from the beginning.' The thing is, kids understand, and particularly at that age, they won't think it odd because adults set rules and, when they want, they change the rules. Starting over allows you to reintroduce yourself and restate expectations.

"And let me make one thing perfectly clear: there is no way you are failing at your job! I have made the exact same mistake as you, and I have known dozens of other teachers who have made that mistake, as well. Namely, moving forward with some preconceived assumptions and learning after the fact that you have blundered. It happens all the time in human relations, and the teacher-student relationship is going to suffer its share of bumps.

"However, being the adult and authority figure, you can fix it up quickly and be right back on track."

Point taken?

Asking for Help

When you are a student-teacher or brand-new to your career, you are expected to be learning. Therefore, don't hesitate for a second to ask somebody for help if you feel that you need it. Of course, any teacher should be willing to ask for help at any point in her career, but it does get harder the longer you are in the classroom. Therefore, if you need some input, now is the time to ask for it.

This goes beyond asking for observations or assessments as I mentioned earlier; it can mean asking for input during collaboration on how to teach a particular standard. Or getting feedback on why your kids aren't understanding how to properly punctuate a sentence. Remember: you can't be observing how things work in other rooms when you are teaching your own students, so you have to *ask*.

Don't expect that other teachers will have perfect answers to your problems. Rather, expect that having a professional conversation with another educator will help your mind process ways to improve. Eventually, you'll find a way that works for you, and asking for help can dramatically speed up the rate of self-discovery. It can also show other teachers that you are not too proud to get input. This can help cement relationships and also make other teachers feel safe coming to *you* for input if they notice you doing something particularly well.

Finally, I'm going to make the plea that, if you are feeling overwhelmed in any aspect of your teaching, do not wait until it is taking a toll on your personal life. Anything that's affecting your personal life will affect your classroom life, as well. Ask for the help that you need before your students suffer the consequences.

Finding a Kindred Spirit

Rest assured, Classroom Caboodle is here for you to provide guidance and insights. However, it's no substitute for finding a fellow teacher with whom you can have frank discussions and – when necessary – commiserate.

This person does not have to be in your school. In fact, you might be expecting a bit much if you think that you will be able to find a kindred soul amongst the staff of a particular school. If you do, great. But hedge your bets by staying in contact with the other graduates of your college education program.

You don't have to restrict your search to other teachers in your grade level or even your specialty. I have had some of my best one-on-one relationships with high school teachers and elementary music teachers. You meet other teachers everywhere you go, especially when you are involved in district-level training. It's much more important to find someone with whom you "click" than someone who perfectly matches the same job description you have.

Look for these people, treasure them, and do your part to keep these relationship going.

Every teacher needs another teacher with whom she can create a conversational "safe zone," where concerns can be discussed and burdens unloaded. You will never be sorry that you have someone – besides your patient partner or spouse – with whom to share your stories.

Staying Healthy

I've made a big deal out of the fact that kids can't afford to lose a year of progress in elementary school, and they really can't. But that's a lot of pressure, isn't it? I can get kind of intense on that topic, I know.

So now I need to take a step back, take a deep breath, and state another fact: Kids won't make *any* progress if their teacher isn't there to teach them. And by "there," I mean completely present, every day, healthy in both mind and body.

School is hard on dedicated teachers - sometimes very hard. Even if you can avoid the illness that comes from exposure to new germs, you will find yourself very tired on Friday afternoons and completely exhausted by the time winter break rolls around. It's not just the physical movement that's necessary to keep your little pack together; it's the mental effort of absorbing new concepts nonstop.

So please: be self-aware and recognize the signs of approaching burnout - that's the ultimate case of "falling down," and it's very hard to get back up from it. There is only one cure for it, and that is adequate time off to decompress and rebuild your strength, attitude, and enthusiasm. How?

- Protect your personal time at home in the evening by avoiding idle chit-chat during the day when you could be correcting papers.

- Protect your personal time on the weekends by setting aside clearly-defined hours to work and not allowing yourself to go beyond that, even if it means your lesson plans aren't perfect and you have to improvise a bit in the classroom. I know you'll be working on the weekend - all teachers do - but you have to set limits and stick with them.

- Protect your personal time during breaks by limiting your projects to a very, very small list. Again, I know you'll need to get some work done, but give yourself a very small bite to chew - you can always take another bite if you find that you have time.

In short, take good care of yourself. That's an order!

Your Adventure Begins

I'm excited for you! Although it seems like a long time ago, I remember setting off on my own teaching adventure like it was yesterday. There have been highs and lows, exultations and frustrations, and enough corrected papers to reach to the moon and back!

But through it all has shone one thing: my students.... my little people. For every moment of heartache or frustration that I have endured, they've given back to me a thousand moments of love and joy.

This, my friends, is what you have to look forward to from this honored profession that you have decided to join. I wish you every bit of luck and good fortune.

Go forth and be awesome!

I'd Love to Hear from You!

I love to hear from my followers. You can always get ahold of me by using the contact form on my website. You'll find it easily enough at ClassroomCaboodle.com. You can also look me up on social media - there are links on my website.

So don't be shy!

Your FREE Resources

Remember, I have set up a page that is only for readers of this book at this link:

www.ClassroomCaboodle.com/NewTeacher

Here is what you'll find there:

- Helpful videos
- Free downloads
- Recommended resources for new teachers
- Discount coupons for my store

I love my teacher readers, and I'm happy to provide these extra items just for you!

Thank You!

I really appreciate your choosing this book - I'm honored that you would consider using my ideas to shape your approach to teaching.

If you like what you've read, then please help me spread the word to other teachers. I would really appreciate it if you would take a moment and leave a review of this book on Amazon.

www.ClassroomCaboodle.com/NewTeacherBook

~ Betsy Weigle

~

You can see all of my books at this page:
www.ClassroomCaboodleBooks.com

Made in the USA
Middletown, DE
19 October 2016